Air Force Records
for Family Historians

Figure 1 A Royal Engineers balloon in South Africa,
1899–1902 (Copy 1/444)

Air Force Records
for Family Historians

William Spencer

PUBLIC RECORD OFFICE

Public Record Office Readers' Guide No. 21

Public Record Office
Kew
Richmond
Surrey TW9 4DU

ISBN 1 873162 93 6

British Library Cataloguing-in-Publication Data
A catalogue record for this book is available from the British Library.

Photograph credits

The frontispiece of the balloon in South Africa, taken by Horace Nicholls, appears courtesy of the Royal Photographic Society, Bath.

The photographs taken from the Royal Aero Club Certificates of A.G. Fox and A.B. Spencer appear courtesy of the Royal Aero Club and the Royal Air Force Museum.

The photographs of A.B. Spencer as a Petty Officer, RNAS and of the RAF Long Service and Good Conduct medal appear courtesy of the author.

Cover: Air Observation pilots' wings (WO 32/13902); officers of 804 Naval Air Squadron (ADM 207/8)

Printed by The Cromwell Press Ltd, Trowbridge, Wilts.

Contents

Foreword

Graham Mottram

About thirty years ago, the American author Alvin Toffler wrote a book called *Future Change*, the subject of which was the way that life had changed in the twentieth century, and how it was likely to change in the future. A central part of his thesis was that it was not the SPEED of change which was creating problems in society, but the ACCELERATION of change. In simplistic terms, things just get faster, faster.

That is certainly true in the history of aviation and aerospace. My father was born a year before Louis Bleriot flew across the Channel, when Britain was still an island. When I was born, jet aircraft were still something of a rarity. My son, a postgraduate student, has never known a world in which man has not walked on the moon. It took several thousand years for man to rise from the ground under control, but little more than another fifty years for him to truly slip the 'surly bonds of earth'. Aviation is a twentieth century phenomenon, and one which has affected all our lives in one way or another. The development of one branch of technology, internal combustion engines for road vehicles for example, led to the Wright brothers being able to construct a viable aero-engine for their pioneering aircraft. Fifty years later, the need to slow heavy aircraft safely on landing led to the design of anti-lock braking systems, now commonplace on cars as ABS. There is no doubt that aviation electronics, or avionics, has contributed massively to the reduction in size and weight of consumer electronics, with the result that many of us have, on our desks, computing power many times greater than that carried by the moon landers of the late 1960s.

It is these same computers which present a threat to more traditional forms of record keeping, and one has to wonder whether the Public Record Office will be able to update this book in fifty years time including, by then, the aviation personnel records of later generations. Or will the later generations have been dealt with on a hard disk, and records deleted when the individual is no longer in the services, or has died and ceased to draw a pension? Will the PRO become a repository of old hard disks, installed in hoary old computers which are the only machines which can read outdated magnetic formats?

Here is the acceleration of change in the recording and preservation of information throughout the twentieth century. The records to which William Spencer offers a clear and lucid guide are not only valuable in terms of their content, but also in terms of their form and style. No clerk in 1900 government service, either civilian or military, would retain his post unless his handwriting was elegant. To modern eyes, copperplate writing is often a little illegible, but it looks lovely on the page. Even if that page is now a little yellow, the official form is a memorial to a bureaucracy inextricably linked to the strict social mores of the time. In our modern world, where awareness of the armed services and their organization is often very low, guides of the nature of this book are essential to researchers who need to find their way to the basic information on great grandfather or uncle's time in the colours.

When one moves further through the century, the typewriter sometimes replaces the clerk's hand. Forms in duplicate or triplicate could only be produced in one way in an operational squadron's office – but how many people under the age of thirty have ever seen carbon paper, let alone used it in a mandraulic typewriter? As the Director of one of the museums listed as an additional source of records of help to the researcher, whether genealogical or historical, I am very aware that archives are in danger of becoming a thing of the past in themselves, or, at the very least, databanks which end almost with a line drawn under a particular date. That date will probably have little historical significance in the wider sense, but will simply be the time when paper was replaced by computer. Archive managers are already being faced with the problem that paper is essentially a self destructive medium, fading and embrittling with age, such that its vital information content is in danger of crumbling into oblivion. Digital imaging will have to come, and we will have to find the funding. So the progress in this century will hopefully allow us to maintain the clerical output of past generations for the use of those in the future.

William Spencer's book is a splendid example of how the PRO itself has progressed. When I first used Chancery Lane nearly thirty years ago, its ethos was only slightly post-Dickensian, and the customer service skills of the staff could be somewhat perfunctory. Today, however, the PRO has a zappy website, and a policy towards accessibility and openness which leads to the production of guides such as this. No matter how hard those of us involved with record management try to ensure 100% retention, there will always be some things which slip through the net. Those records which survive now and into the future provide a feast of information and hopefully pleasure to those who research in them. If your ancestors served in the British and Commonwealth air forces, you have a very good chance of discovering what they did, and this book will help you to discover those facts more quickly.

Graham Mottram
Director of the Fleet Air Arm Museum

Preface

Aviation has always been a great interest of mine. From when I had a flight in an Auster on my seventh birthday, to 13 years as an aircraft engineer in the Fleet Air Arm, to being Military Specialist at the Public Record Office (PRO), aircraft and the people who flew and maintained them have always been an enthusiasm and continue to be part of my working life.

As military aviation is a relatively new part of military history, so the associated records held by the PRO are also relatively new, especially considering the age of the greater part of the archive. The study of military history, especially the First World War period, is extremely popular, not just with genealogists but also with those who have an interest in the varied aspects of warfare and military service. This guide stems from a number of varied interests in different aspects of military aviation but primarily from a desire to see all of the salient information put into one place.

There are numerous people who deserve thanks for the variety of help, information and guidance I have received: Aidan Lawes for commissioning the guide and Anne Kilminster and the PRO Publications Department for their help in creating the finished book; Hugh Alexander for his assistance with regard to illustrations; the archival staff at the Fleet Air Arm Museum, Moira Gittos, Jan Keoghane and Jerry Shore, for help with Arthur Bedward Spencer; the archival staff at the RAF Museum, Simon Moody and Andrew Whitmarsh, for help with Royal Aero Club Certificates and their own archival holdings; Dave Morris for the loan of various items relating to Alan Geoffrey Fox; Paul Baillie for his insight into the surviving RAF honours and awards files. My colleague Lee Oliver must also be thanked for producing the list of abbreviations.

Special thanks must go to Graham Mottram, Director of the Fleet Air Arm Museum, for writing the foreword.

My final thanks must as always go to Kate, Lucy and Alice for allowing me the time to produce yet 'another book, Daddy'!

Introduction

Studying the flying services has always been popular. The careers of famous pilots, and indeed most aircrew, have always been closely scrutinised. However, now that the records of service of men of the RFC (Royal Flying Corps), RNAS (Royal Naval Air Service), and some of the RAF (Royal Air Force) up to given dates have been released, so those personnel who were a very important yet neglected part of aviation history can now be studied. Together with many operational records, which have been available for a number of years, it is now possible to study complete aspects of aviation from high command to many of the individuals who took part.

This guide consolidates all the records relating to individuals into one place. It also provides information about records which were either not available or which were not covered in depth when *RAF Records in the PRO* was published. From the pioneering Royal Engineer balloonists of 1878, to the operational records of the RAF, the Fleet Air Arm (FAA) and the Army Air Corps (AAC) in the post-1945 period, this guide brings together the key records created by the various government departments involved in the administration of the flying services and their personnel.

Using the PRO and accessing the records held there is now far easier than even five years ago. With the advent of the on-line catalogue, it is possible not only to identify records before you arrive at the PRO, but also to carry out keyword searches of the catalogue ('On-line Lists'), thereby letting the computer do the work of turning pages to find the records required. See the 'Using the PRO' section in this guide for more information about the on-line catalogue.

Contrary to popular belief, archives never stand still. Although there are numerous operational records available up to the 1960s, the records of service of men and women who saw service after the early 1920s are still held by the Ministry of Defence (MOD). Consequently when the records of service that are currently less than 75 years old are released, so the study of aviation and the men and women who were part of it will continue. Records of service are held for 75 years by the MOD for administrative purposes.

The format of this guide is such that, beyond placing each of the flying services into its historical context, it concentrates on providing guidance about the records where information about individuals may be found.

Using the PRO

The Public Record Office is the national repository for government records in the UK. Its main site at Kew holds the surviving records of government back to the Domesday Book (1086) and beyond. The records already occupy more than 170 km of shelving and are increasing every day. The PRO at Kew is usually the best place to go to search for an ancestor in the armed forces.

Public Record Office
Kew
Richmond
Surrey TW9 4DU
General telephone: 020 8876 3444
Telephone number for enquiries: 020 8392 5200
Telephone number for advance ordering of documents
(with exact references only): 020 8382 5260
Internet: http://www.pro.gov.uk/

Opening times (closed Sundays, public holidays, and for annual stockstaking)

Monday	9.00 a.m. to 5 p.m.
Tuesday	10 a.m. to 7 p.m.
Wednesday	9.00 a.m. to 5 p.m.
Thursday	9.00 a.m. to 7 p.m.
Friday	9.00 a.m. to 5 p.m.
Saturday	9.30 a.m. to 5 p.m.

Note that the last time for ordering documents is 4 p.m. on Mondays, Wednesdays and Fridays; 4.30 p.m. on Tuesdays and Thursdays, and 2.30 p.m. on Saturdays.

The PRO is about ten minutes' walk from Kew Gardens Underground Station, which is on London Transport's District Line, as well as the North London Line Silverlink Metro service. For motorists it is just off the South Circular Road (A205). There is adequate parking, as well as a public restaurant, bookshop, self-service lockers and extensive library. New in April 2000 is the Education and Visitor Centre.

The PRO can be a confusing place on your first visit, but staff are knowledgable and friendly and happy to help. No appointment is needed to visit, but you will need a reader's ticket to gain access to research areas. To obtain a ticket take with you a full UK driving licence or UK banker's card, or a passport if you are a British citizen, and your passport or national identity card if you are not a British citizen.

To protect the documents, each one of which is unique, security in the reading rooms is tight. You are only permitted to take a notebook and notes (up to six loose sheets) into the reading rooms, where eating, drinking and smoking are not permitted.

The PRO 'On-line'

As well as giving information on where the PRO is, opening times and how to gain access, the PRO website gives details about popular records, including leaflets and lists of researchers. Most importantly the website allows readers to access the PRO catalogue (class lists).

The catalogue (class lists) can be searched by using up to three keywords, and if you know them, the letter code and class, where records are known to exist.

Follow these simple steps to identify the documents you require:

1. Locate the catalogue.
2. Click on *Search Catalogue*.
3. Type in up to three keywords (one in each box) and, if known, the letter code and class boxes (optional).
4. Click on *Search*.

The computer will then search for classes where records of interest may be held. Click on *Description* for further information, or respond to the message 'to search for the word . . . within individual document descriptions use *Search Documents*' (in red). However, it is possible that no documents, using your search terms will be listed. If so, click on *Search Documents*. The computer will then list any documents which use the search term(s) you listed, in their document descriptions. If it finds any, it will list them. (Please note that you cannot view the documents themselves alone.)

Organization of military flying up to 1914

1.1 The Royal Engineers and their balloons

Although the use of balloons was discussed by the War Office at least as early as 1804 (WO 30/71), effective use of them only started in 1878, when a number of experiments were conducted at Woolwich Arsenal. These experiments were accompanied by the creation of a Balloon Equipment Store, and by 1879 the Royal Engineers were using a few officers and men to conduct further trials.

After balloons took part in army manoeuvres in 1880 and 1882, a balloon detachment accompanied the Bechuanaland expedition in 1884 and another detachment went to eastern Sudan. (See Section 8.1 for operational records.)

The Balloon Section Royal Engineers was authorized in May 1890. The Balloon Equipment Store which had been at Chatham since 1883 was now separated from the Balloon Factory and School, which moved to Farnborough. The Balloon Equipment Store remained at Chatham as the depot but in 1892 moved, along with the Balloon Factory, to Aldershot, where it became the School of Ballooning.

During the Boer War, Nos 1, 2 and 3 sections, RE Balloon Section served in South Africa, whilst No. 4 section saw service in China. (See Section 8.1 for operational records.)

After the Wright Flyer (the first powered aeroplane) had flown in 1903, a developing interest in aeroplanes began to influence the Balloon Section to such a degree that changes were inevitable. After experiments with both airships and aeroplanes between 1908 and 1911, the Air Battalion of the Royal Engineers was authorized in February 1911, with the new battalion becoming effective from 1 April of the same year.

As the new Air Battalion grew and aircraft of all types illustrated their military potential, so the size and status of the Air Battalion was investigated by the Committee of Imperial Defence. Britain had been left behind by a number of European countries which had already created separate air services. A Technical Sub-Committee of the Committee of Imperial Defence eventually concluded that a separate air service was needed and the product of these conclusions was the creation of the Royal Flying Corps on 13 May 1912.

1.2 The Royal Flying Corps

The establishment of the Royal Flying Corps on 13 May 1912 finally acknowledged the importance of military aviation (CAB 38/20). Numerous records concerning the RFC and its expansion and development can be found in AIR 1, from the recruitment and training of RFC personnel to the design, manufacture and purchase of aircraft and the establishment of units and their preparation for war.

1.3 The Royal Naval Air Service

The Royal Naval Air Service did not really exist as a separate service by name until July 1914. Before then the RNAS was the Naval Wing of the Royal Flying Corps, staffed by officers and men who had volunteered from other branches of the service.

Naval interest in aviation dates back to 1908, when Captain R.H.S. Bacon, Director of Naval Ordnance, put forward a proposal for the construction of a rigid airship to be used for fleet reconnaissance.

There are numerous sources, both primary and secondary, which can provide details relating to naval aviation. By far the most useful secondary source is *Documents relating to the Naval Air Service 1908–1918*, Captain S.W. Roskill, ed. (Naval Records Society, 1969). This is full of PRO document references and a copy is available in the PRO Library.

A file listing the numbers of officers and men in the RFC Naval Wing at Farnborough in July 1913 can be found in AIR 1/763/204/4/196.

2 Organization of the Royal Flying Corps, Royal Naval Air Service and Royal Air Force up to 1918

2.1 The Royal Flying Corps

With the outbreak of the First World War, the RFC was at last given the opportunity to show what they could do and how aircraft could contribute to the battlefield.

The structure of the RFC altered as the size of the British Expeditionary Force changed. As early as November 1914, the RFC was formed into two wings of two squadrons each: No. 1 Wing served the First Army and No. 2 Wing the Second Army. As the Third, Fourth and Fifth Armies were created so the RFC adapted itself accordingly. In August 1915 each army became supported by an RFC brigade made up of two aeroplane wings and a balloon wing. This structure remained until the end of the war.

2.2 The Royal Naval Air Service

Although there was a naval wing of the RFC prior to 1914, it was not until July of that year that the Royal Naval Air Service became a separate entity. Personnel strength of the RNAS between August 1914 and March 1918 can be found in AIR 1/626/17/60.

Rough notes on the early development of the RNAS covering the period 1912–17 can be found in AIR 1/625/17/1, and a short history of the service in AIR 1/682/21/13/2226.

2.3 The Royal Air Force and Women's Royal Air Force

The Royal Air Force and Women's Royal Air Force (WRAF) were formed on 1 April 1918. Manpower for the RAF came from the Royal Flying Corps and Royal Naval Air Service. Many of the women were new entrants but some did come from the Women's Army Auxiliary Corps.

The basic operational structure of the RAF was the same as that of the pre-April 1918 RFC. However, the biggest operational change to take place after the formation of the RAF was the creation of the Independent Air Force, whose task was to carry out strategic bombing of targets in Germany.

Historical notes about the WRAF can be found in AIR 1/681/21/13/2212.

The development and operations of the RFC, RNAS and RAF during the First World War are covered in the *War in the Air* by Sir W. Raleigh and H.E. Jones.

3 Organization of the Royal Air Force, Fleet Air Arm, and Glider Pilot Regiment and Army Air Corps from 1919 to the 1960s

3.1 The Royal Air Force

Soon after the First World War, and especially after the signing of the Treaty of Versailles in 1919, the manpower of the RAF started to be reduced. Once Germany had been defeated an air force of such size was seen as unnecessary. By January 1920, the RAF had demobilized over 250,000 men. However, at the same time, new tasks for the RAF were being considered. By far the most important task the RAF was to undertake between 1919 and 1939 was that of colonial policing. The best book on this subject is *Air Power and Colonial Control* by David Omissi.

As the RAF was almost a wartime creation, the manpower within it were nearly all wartime volunteers only. In 1919 plans for a permanent RAF were drawn up and in subsequent years many of the administrative structures and institutions as we know them today were created.

Between 1919 and 1939 many changes took place with regard to how the RAF operated its aircraft. From the First World War period squadrons, wings and brigades became squadrons, groups and commands. The United Kingdom was split into two commands, known as area commands, which were split into inland and coastal areas, each with numbered groups representing different parts of the country. These two commands were the two key operational parts of the Air Defence of Great Britain (ADGB).

Two further commands in the United Kingdom at this time were Cranwell and Halton Commands, responsible for the training of officers and airmen respectively.

Outside the United Kingdom, overseas commands in various parts of the Empire continued the colonial policing role which prior to 1914 had been solely undertaken by the army. India, Iraq, Palestine, Middle East and Mediterranean were all overseas commands between 1919 and 1939.

The biggest changes to RAF structures to occur before outbreak of the Second World War were the abandonment of the Air Defence of Great Britain Command and the formation of separate commands relative to the task each aircraft type was allocated to do. In place of the ADGB came Fighter Command, Bomber Command, Coastal Command and others including, for example, those responsible for balloons, training, co-operation with the army and maintenance. Operational Record Books (ORBs) and other command papers for these organizations can be found amongst the AIR record classes.

Changes to manpower requirements between the wars saw the creation of the Auxiliary Air Force (AAF) in October 1925 and the Royal Air Force Volunteer Reserve just prior to the outbreak of the Second World War. Auxiliary Air Force squadrons saw considerable success during the Second World War. AAF squadrons were numbered in the 500 and 600 numerical range. Further details can be found in *RAF Squadrons* by Jefford.

Creation of an RAF nursing service, the Princess Mary's Royal Air Force Nursing Service, occurred in 1921. Details concerning its establishment can be found in AIR 2/93.

Operational records of the inter war years can be found in Section 8.4.2.

The advent of the Second World War saw the RAF adapt to the operational and strategic needs of the conflict. Various changes took place, including the creation of special units, such as 617 Squadron, and whole air forces such as the 2nd Tactical Air Force (2 TAF). For operational records of the Second World War period see Section 8.4.3.

Beyond the changes to command structure and the creation of various squadrons during the Second World War, the single most important creation of this period was the RAF Regiment described below.

3.1.1 The RAF Regiment

The Royal Air Force Regiment was originally formed as the RAF Aerodrome Defence Corps in 1942. Created to protect airfields, the RAF Regiment has served in numerous operational theatres around the world. Records concerning the regiment can be found in AIR 2, Series B, Code 90, with specific files AIR 2/4880 and AIR 2/5378 concerning its formation and early history. Further files concerning manpower, its formation and role, and another history are in AIR 20/2027, 3658 and 4032, respectively. Operational records of the RAF Regiment are discussed in Chapter 8.

Further exploits of the RAF Regiment and its forebears can be found in *In Adversity – Exploits of Gallantry and Awards to the RAF Regiment and its Associated Forces 1921–1995* by Squadron Leader N.G. Tucker, RAF.

3.1.2 The RAF since 1945

As occurred after the end of the First World War, the RAF has undergone a number administrative and structural changes since 1945. As the British Empire has gradually shrunk, so the global character of British military commitment has changed. From being the main deliverer of Britain's nuclear deterrent until the 1960s, the roles and responsibilities of the RAF have likewise continued to change.

For those carrying out research into the activities of the RAF since 1945, only the operational records and records relating to awards are so far in the public domain. Changes to RAF commands since 1945 are not the responsibility of this guide.

3.2 The Fleet Air Arm

After the First World War the RAF took control of all aspects of aviation, although, of course, the Royal Navy was responsible for the aircraft carrying ships. Although the Fleet Air Arm (FAA) was created officially in name in 1924, administrative control of naval aviation and naval aircraft was the responsibility of the RAF and was only returned to the Royal Navy in 1937. The complexities of this inter-service rivalry are best explored by reading Stephen Roskill's *Naval Policy between the Wars*. The restoration of Admiralty control of naval aviation was a result of the Inskip Report, a copy of which can be found in AIR 8/223.

The majority of FAA squadrons are numbered between 700 and 899, those in the 700 range being second line units and those in the 800 range, front line. A number of other numerical ranges have also been used. For a brief history of all the FAA squadrons, see *Squadrons of the Fleet Air Arm* by Ray Sturtivant.

As has similarly happened to the Army and RAF after 1945, the FAA has diminished in size but not effectiveness, and has been involved in numerous operations around the world.

A history of the RNAS and FAA covering the period 1903–45 can be found in AIR 20/6349. Further histories of the FAA can be found in ADM 335.

3.3 The Glider Pilot Regiment and Army Air Corps

Created as the direct result of an instruction made by Winston Churchill in June 1940, the Glider Pilot Regiment (GPR) and its administering corps, the Army Air Corps, were established in February 1942. The Army Air Corps was also responsible for the Parachute Regiment and Special Air Service, both of which are outside the remit of this book. Churchill's instructions for the creation of the Glider Pilot Regiment, together with some operational records, can be found in WO 233.

The use of gliders was abandoned soon after the end of the Second World War and the Glider Pilot Regiment was disbanded in 1957. The Army Air Corps was disbanded in 1950 but the need for an army corps to be responsible for aviation led to the Army Air Corps being reformed at the same time as the Glider Pilot Regiment was disbanded. Records concerning the Army Air Corps can be found in WO 295.

4 Royal Engineers Balloon Section records of service

The records discussed in this chapter concern the personnel of the RE Balloon Section, its forebears and successors up to 12 May 1912 only. Records of service of the RFC, RNAS and RAF are dealt with in Chapters 5, 6 and 7 respectively.

4.1 Officers

The first type of record to approach when researching any officers who served in the British army after 1760 is the Army Lists. These lists are available in the Microfilm Reading Room. They appear in a variety of formats (yearly, half yearly, quarterly and monthly), each with its own particular type of information. Each volume is internally indexed, with the number alongside the name representing a page reference within the volume. In many cases officers may appear on more than one page, especially if they are of senior rank. The Army Lists contain gradation lists arranged in order of seniority, i.e. date of promotion to a given rank. These can provide more information about appointments and courses attended. The 'War Services' sections provide brief details about the military operations an officer was involved in, together with information about medals and awards.

Also of use, although not officially created by the state, are the Hart's Army Lists 1879–1915. These lists contain information which is not readily available in the 'official' Army List. The biographical papers created by Hart covering the period 1838–75 and relating to many of the officers found in these lists can be found in WO 211. Hart's Army Lists are available in the Microfilm Reading Room and Library.

A published list of RE officers, the *Roll of Officers of the Corps of Royal Engineers from 1660–1898*, is available in the Library.

Records of service of RE officers kept by the War Office can be found in WO 25/3913–3920; information within these records covers the period 1796–1937. These records are arranged by date of commission and they contain biographical data concerning both the officer and, if he had them, his wife and children, including dates of promotions and appointments, campaigns and medals and his nominated next of kin.

Reference	Date
WO 25/3913	1796–1860
WO 25/3914	1860–1921
WO 25/3915	1873–1928
WO 25/3916	1886–1918
WO 25/3917	1885–1937
WO 25/3918	1895–1935
WO 25/3919	1904–1915
WO 25/3920	1876–1915 includes Supplementary Reserve

Records of service formerly held by the Royal Engineers can be found in WO 76/15–23. These records cover the period 1866–1907 and are arranged by Royal Engineer division, with each volume internally indexed. However, these records only concern RE (Militia) (part-time) officers.

War Office: Records of Officers' Service, Royal Engineers (M)

Reference	Date	Division
WO 76/15	1879–1907	Falmouth
WO 76/16	1880–1906	Harwich
WO 76/17	1872–1897	Harwich
WO 76/18	1892–1906	Humber
WO 76/19	1866–1905	Medway
WO 76/20	1882–1906	Milford Haven
WO 76/21	1874–1906	Plymouth
WO 76/22	1896–1905	Thames
WO 76/23	1888–1904	Western

4.2 Other ranks

As the Royal Engineers did not embark upon experiments with balloons until 1878, the records of service of men involved in pioneering British military aviation are scarce. Although the process to find such records is easy, in many cases, unless you know that an individual serving in the Royal Engineers was involved in ballooning, then the outward signs on a record of service do not necessarily help.

The records of service of those men of the British Army who were discharged to pension up to 1913, or who served on a short service engagement which expired between 1883 and 1913, are in the record class WO 97. These records are arranged in chronological sections covering 1873–82, 1883–1900 and 1900–1913, with each section arranged in alphabetical order. Prior to 1883 each chronological section is arranged by regiment or corps. After 1883 each chronological section represents the whole army and is not broken into regimental or corps groups. The piece ranges of the sections are:

Date	Reference	Coverage
1873–1882	WO 97/1849–1857	Specifically Royal Engineers
1883–1900	WO 97/2172–4231	All of the army
1900–1913	WO 97/4232–6322	All of the army
1900–1913	WO 97/6323–6354	Supplementary series
1843–1899	WO 97/6355–6383	Supplementary series

The records in this class are likely to provide some of the following information:

- physical description at attestation and discharge
- date of attestation and discharge
- dates of promotions
- medical and disciplinary histories
- dates of overseas and campaign service
- details about medals
- name of wife and children (if any), together with marriage and baptism dates
- intended place of residence on discharge.

4.3 Case studies

4.3.1 Gerard Moore Heath

Gerard Heath was born on 7 June 1863, son of Admiral Sir Leopold and Mary Heath. After being educated at Wimbledon and the Royal Military Academy, Woolwich, he was commissioned into the Royal Engineers in February 1882. In a career that was to last until 1919, it was as early as 1884 that Heath encountered balloons with his participation in the Bechuanaland operations.

Promoted to Captain in 1890, Heath went on to see further operational service in India in 1895. Gaining his majority on 4 October 1899, he soon sailed with a large part of the British Army to South Africa. It was in South Africa, specifically during the defence of Ladysmith, that Heath was reacquainted with balloons by commanding the balloon section which was part of the besieged garrison.

For his service in South Africa, Heath was given a brevet promotion to Lieutenant Colonel and made a Companion of the Distinguished Service Order.

Promoted to full Lieutenant Colonel in 1906, postings to India and Burma were followed in 1912 by a return to South Africa as Temporary Brigadier-General, General Staff.

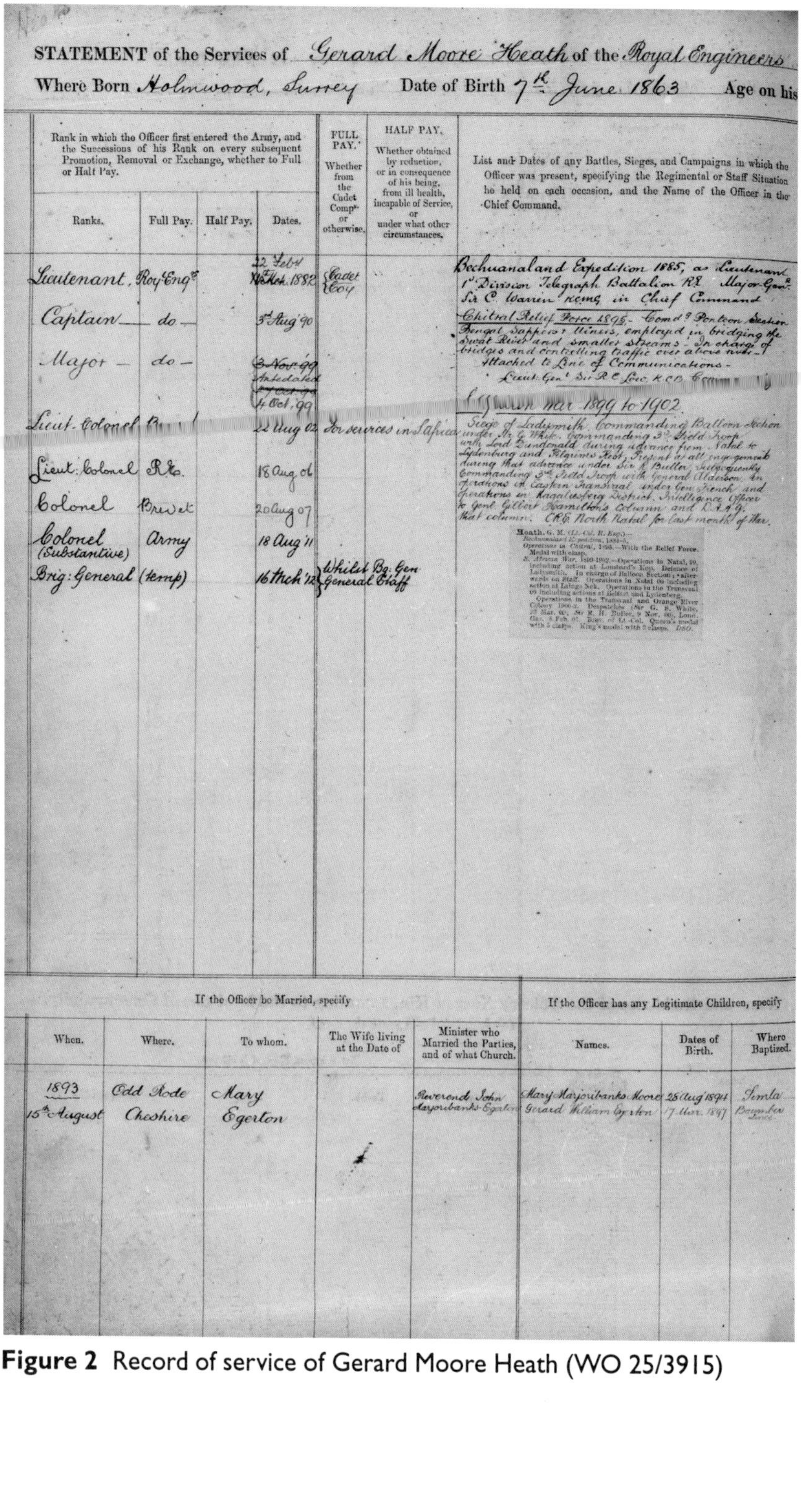

STATEMENT of the Services of Gerard Moore Heath of the Royal Engineers

Where Born Holmwood, Surrey Date of Birth 7th June 1863 Age on his

Ranks.	Full Pay.	Half Pay.	Dates.	FULL PAY. Whether from the Cadet Compy. or otherwise.	HALF PAY. Whether obtained by reduction, or in consequence of his being, from ill health, incapable of Service, or under what other circumstances.	List and Dates of any Battles, Sieges, and Campaigns in which the Officer was present, specifying the Regimental or Staff Situation he held on each occasion, and the Name of the Officer in the Chief Command.
Lieutenant	Roy Engrs		22 Feby 1882	Cadet Coy		Bechuanaland Expedition 1885, as Lieutenant 1st Division Telegraph Battalion RE Major-Genl Sir C. Warren KCMG in Chief Command
Captain	do		5th Aug 90			Chitral Relief Force 1895 – Comdg Pontoon Section Bengal Sappers & Miners, employed in bridging the Swat River and smaller streams – In charge of bridges and controlling traffic over above river – Attached to Line of Communications – Lieut Genl Sir R C Low KCB Comg
Major	do		~~3 Nov 99~~ Antedated 4 Oct 99			[illegible] war 1899 to 1902
Lieut-Colonel	B[illegible]		22 Aug 02	For services in S Africa		Siege of Ladysmith Commanding Balloon Section under Sir G White. Commanding 3rd Field Troop with Lord Dundonald during advance from Natal to Lydenburg and Pilgrims Rest. Present at all engagements during that advance under Sir R Buller. Subsequently Commanding 3rd Field Troop with General Alderson. In operations in Eastern Transvaal under Gen French and operations in Kaapmuiden District. Intelligence Officer to Genl Gilbert Hamilton's Column and D.A.A.G. that column. CRE North Natal for last month of War.
Lieut: Colonel	R.E.		18 Aug 06			
Colonel	Brevet		20 Aug 07			
Colonel (Substantive)	Army		18 Aug 11			
Brig: General	(temp)		16 Mch 12	Whilst Bg: Gen General Staff		

Heath, G. M. (Lt.-Col. R. Eng.)—
Bechuanaland Expedition, 1884-5.
Operations in Chitral, 1895.—With the Relief Force. Medal with clasp.
S. African War, 1899-1902.—Operations in Natal, 99, including action at Lombard's Kop. Defence of Ladysmith. In charge of Balloon Section; afterwards on Staff. Operations in Natal 00 including action at Laing's Nek. Operations in the Transvaal 00 including actions at Belfast and Lydenberg.
Operations in the Transvaal and Orange River Colony 1900-2. Despatches (Sir G. S. White, 23 Mar. 00; Sir R. H. Buller, 9 Nov. 00), Lond. Gaz. 8 Feb. 01. Brev. of Lt.-Col. Queen's medal with 5 clasps. King's medal with 2 clasps. DSO.

If the Officer be Married, specify: When.	Where.	To whom.	The Wife living at the Date of	Minister who Married the Parties, and of what Church.	If the Officer has any Legitimate Children, specify: Names.	Dates of Birth.	Where Baptized.
1893 15th August	Odd Rode Cheshire	Mary Egerton		Reverend John Marjoribanks Egerton	Mary Marjoribanks Moore	28 Aug 1894	Simla
					Gerard William Egerton	17 Mar 1897	Bombay

Figure 2 Record of service of Gerard Moore Heath (WO 25/3915)

197

292

with a Record of such other Particulars as may be useful in case of his Death.

first entrance into the Army *18 Years 9 Months* Religious Persuasion *Church of England*

Instances in which the Officer has distinguished himself by Gallant or Skilful Conduct; when, where, and on what occasion and whether noticed in General Orders.	Wounds received in Action, specifying when, where, and on what occasion; what Grant of Pay has been received; Rate of Pension, Date, and whether permanent or temporary.	Titles, Honorary Distinctions, and Medals obtained; and if conferred for any specified Service, when, and on what occasion.	SERVICE AT HOME.					SERVICE ABROAD.				
			Period.				Stations.	Period.				Stations.
			From	To	Yrs.	Days.		From	To	Yrs.	Days.	
Mentioned by Brig. Telegraphs in despatch of Sir C Warren		D.S.O. for South Africa (Lon. Gaz. 19/4/01)	4 Mch 1882	21 Apl '82	.	116	Leave	29 Jan 85	22 Dec 85	.	328	Bechuanaland
		Brevet of Lt Col for S Africa	23 Apl 1882	5 June 84	2	42	S.M.E. Chatham	23 Nov 87	31 Jan 91	3	70	India (Bengal)
Mentioned in letter from C in C to Govr of India			6 June 84	28 Jun 86	.	227	Aldershot	29 Apr 93	21 June 96	2	266	India
Commended in despatch No 26 dated Simla 11.1.96		Medal & Clasp for S Africa	28 Dec 86	30 Sept 86	.	282		30 Sept 99	10 Dec 01	2	72	Natal (Balloon Sect)
		Medal & Clasp for Chitral	1 Oct 86	30 Sept 87	1	.	2nd Decr Tel Bn	11 Dec 01	5 June 02	.	177	S Africa (D. K.?)
Mentioned in despatch of Lieut Gen Sir G White CB South Africa 23/3/00 (Lon Gaz 8/2/01)		Queens Jubilee Medal	1 Oct 87	22 Nov 87	.	53	Aldershot	19 Oct 07	8 Dec 11	4	51	India
		Medal with 2 Clasps and Kings Medal with 2 Clasps for South Africa	1st Feb 91	31 Jan 92	2	0	Staff LE	16 Mch 12	20 Sept 14	2	189	South Africa
Mentioned in despatch of Sir Redvers Buller South Africa 9 11 00 (Lon Gaz 8/2/01)			1st Feb 93	31 Mch 93	.	59	W.O. Office LE	7 May 15	5 Nov 15	.	182	France
			1st Apl 93	24 Apl 93	.	14	Leave LE	8 Nov 15	31 Oct 17	1	360	do
		CB (Lon Gaz 14/5/16)	25 Apl 93	13 Aug 93	.	121	Aldershot LE	1 Nov 17	17 May 19	1	197	do
			24 Aug 93	28 Apl 93	.	46	Leave LE					
			22 June 96	29 Sept 99	3	100	Aldershot					
			8 June 02	10 June 02	.	3	awaiting orders					
			9 June 02	10 June 02	.	2	S.M.E.					
			11 June 02		4	.	do (Instrn)					
			11 June 06	19 July 06	.	39	D.F.W. Office					
			20 July 06	19 Sept 06	.	51	S.M.E. Chatham					
			10 Sept 06	18 Oct 07	1	39	London Dist					
			9 Dec 11	15 Mch 12	.	97	Half pay					
			21 Sept 14	6 May 15	.	228						
			26 May 19	2 Dec 19	.	251	Half pay					

Name and Residence of the Officer's Next of Kin, according to the legal ties of Consanguinity.

(To be inserted with particular care.)

Name.	Degree of Relationship.	Latest known Place of Residence.			
		County.	Parish.	Town.	Street and No.
Admiral Sir Leopold G. Heath KCB	Father	Surrey	Capel	Dorking	Anstie Grange Holmwood Surrey
Mary Heath	Wife		With husband		
G.E. Heath Esq	Brother		Lloyds Royal Exchange E.C.		} as 1st

During the First World War, Heath served initially as Inspector of Royal Engineers, followed by appointment as Chief Engineer, First Army and promotion to Temporary Major-General in November 1915. Promotion to substantive Major-General for distinguished service in the field followed and he was appointed Engineer-in-Chief to the British Armies in the field in November 1917, an appointment he was to hold until the end of the war.

Heath was further decorated for his services during the war by being made a Companion of the Most Honourable Order of the Bath (CB) in 1916 and he was knighted in 1919, when he was made a Knight Commander of the Most Distinguished Order of St Michael and St George (KCMG). Sir Gerard Moore Heath, KCMG, CB, DSO, RE, retired from the army in December 1919, and died in January 1929.

The records of service of G.M. Heath can be found in WO 25/3915 and WO 374/32333. A copy of Heath's record in WO 25/3915 can be seen in Figure 2.

4.3.2 Charles Robertson

Charles Robertson was born in Lambeth, Surrey, in 1867 and joined the Royal Engineers as a bugler, aged 14, in 1881. From his record of service there is no outward sign that Charles was ever involved with balloons. It is only when you delve deeper that a connection with aviation appears.

On enlistment Robertson was described as 5'3¾" tall, with a fair complexion, blue eyes and brown hair. After attending a telegraphy course in November 1882, home service continued, with little to report.

Promoted to Sapper in 1884, he left the country for his first overseas posting to Egypt and the Sudan on 16 February 1885. On this first journey overseas, Robertson was also to see his only active service, around the Red Sea port of Suakin, which resulted in him receiving the Egypt Medal with Suakin 1885 clasp and Khedive's Star 1884–6. It was whilst verifying these medals that the connection with the RE Balloon Section was confirmed by his appearance on their medal roll in WO 100/64 ff80.

Robertson returned to England in July 1885, and another course in telegraphy is noted in November 1887. With this new qualification, promotion to Lance Corporal followed in January 1887, 2nd Corporal in May 1887 and then to Corporal and Sergeant in May and December, respectively, both in the year 1888.

During this period of Home Service, Charles Robertson married Florence Jane Davis at Holy Trinity Church, Plymouth on 15 February 1892. Two children were born before Robertson's next overseas posting: Gladys Florence on 29 November 1892 and Charles Stewart on 31 January 1894.

The birth of Charles Stewart Robertson occurred just before his father went on his second and last overseas posting a two and a half year spell of garrison duty in Halifax, Nova Scotia. Shortly after his arrival in Halifax, Sergeant Robertson was promoted to Company Sergeant Major on 1 July 1894.

Returning to England on 29 November 1897, his final promotion, to Quarter Master Sergeant, occurred on 8 March 1898.

Quarter Master Sergeant Charles Robertson, RE, was finally discharged from the army on 28 January 1906. His appearance was very similar to that when he enlisted but he was now 5' 8"! His intended place of residence on discharge was 27 Anson Place, St Judes, Plymouth. Charles Robertson died on 1 July 1951, aged 84, at Gillingham in Kent.

All of this detail came from his record of service in WO 97/5790, which can be seen in Figure 3.

Research tips

1. RE Officers should always have entries in the Army List. The records in WO 25 are arranged by initial commission date, which can be obtained from the Army Lists.

2. The records of service of RE other ranks who left the service before 1913 should be in the record class WO 97, which is arranged alphabetically.

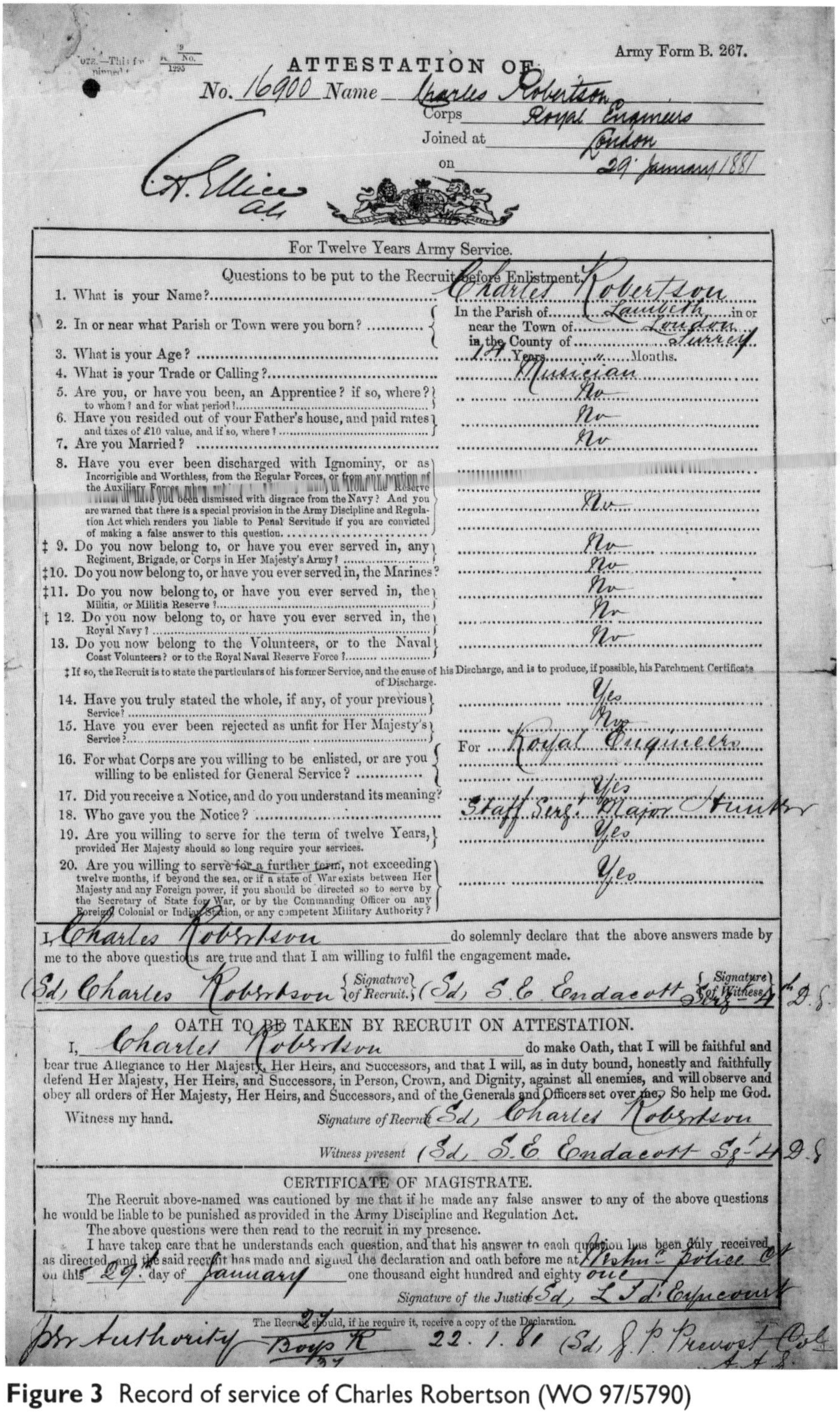

Army Form B. 267.

ATTESTATION OF

No. 16900 Name Charles Robertson

Corps Royal Engineers

Joined at London

on 29 January 1881

C. H. Ellice

For Twelve Years Army Service.

Questions to be put to the Recruit before Enlistment.

1. What is your Name? ... Charles Robertson
2. In or near what Parish or Town were you born? ... In the Parish of Lambeth in or near the Town of London in the County of Surrey
3. What is your Age? ... 19 Years ... Months.
4. What is your Trade or Calling? ... Musician
5. Are you, or have you been, an Apprentice? if so, where? to whom? and for what period? ... No
6. Have you resided out of your Father's house, and paid rates and taxes of £10 value, and if so, where? ... No
7. Are you Married? ... No
8. Have you ever been discharged with Ignominy, or as Incorrigible and Worthless, from the Regular Forces, or from any portion of the Auxiliary Forces ... Reserve ... dismissed with disgrace from the Navy? And you are warned that there is a special provision in the Army Discipline and Regulation Act which renders you liable to Penal Servitude if you are convicted of making a false answer to this question. ... No
‡ 9. Do you now belong to, or have you ever served in, any Regiment, Brigade, or Corps in Her Majesty's Army? ... No
‡10. Do you now belong to, or have you ever served in, the Marines? ... No
‡11. Do you now belong to, or have you ever served in, the Militia, or Militia Reserve? ... No
‡ 12. Do you now belong to, or have you ever served in, the Royal Navy? ... No
13. Do you now belong to the Volunteers, or to the Naval Coast Volunteers? or to the Royal Naval Reserve Force? ... No

‡ If so, the Recruit is to state the particulars of his former Service, and the cause of his Discharge, and is to produce, if possible, his Parchment Certificate of Discharge.

14. Have you truly stated the whole, if any, of your previous Service? ... Yes
15. Have you ever been rejected as unfit for Her Majesty's Service? ... No
16. For what Corps are you willing to be enlisted, or are you willing to be enlisted for General Service? ... For Royal Engineers
17. Did you receive a Notice, and do you understand its meaning? ... Yes
18. Who gave you the Notice? ... Staff Sergt Major Hunter
19. Are you willing to serve for the term of twelve Years, provided Her Majesty should so long require your services. ... Yes
20. Are you willing to serve for a further term, not exceeding twelve months, if beyond the sea, or if a state of War exists between Her Majesty and any Foreign power, if you should be directed so to serve by the Secretary of State for War, or by the Commanding Officer on any Foreign Colonial or Indian Station, or any competent Military Authority? ... Yes

I, Charles Robertson do solemnly declare that the above answers made by me to the above questions are true and that I am willing to fulfil the engagement made.

(Sd) Charles Robertson {Signature of Recruit.} (Sd) S. E. Endacott Sergt 4 D. S. {Signature of Witness.}

OATH TO BE TAKEN BY RECRUIT ON ATTESTATION.

I, Charles Robertson do make Oath, that I will be faithful and bear true Allegiance to Her Majesty, Her Heirs, and Successors, and that I will, as in duty bound, honestly and faithfully defend Her Majesty, Her Heirs, and Successors, in Person, Crown, and Dignity, against all enemies, and will observe and obey all orders of Her Majesty, Her Heirs, and Successors, and of the Generals and Officers set over me. So help me God.

Witness my hand.

Signature of Recruit (Sd) Charles Robertson

Witness present (Sd) S. E. Endacott Sgt 4 D. S.

CERTIFICATE OF MAGISTRATE.

The Recruit above-named was cautioned by me that if he made any false answer to any of the above questions he would be liable to be punished as provided in the Army Discipline and Regulation Act.

The above questions were then read to the recruit in my presence.

I have taken care that he understands each question, and that his answer to each question has been duly received as directed, and the said recruit has made and signed the declaration and oath before me at Metropn police Ct on this 29th day of January one thousand eight hundred and eighty one

Signature of the Justice (Sd) L. T. d'Eyncourt

The Recruit should, if he require it, receive a copy of the Declaration.

per Authority 27 Boys R 27 22. 1. 81 (Sd) J. P. Prevost Col A. A. G.

Figure 3 Record of service of Charles Robertson (WO 97/5790)

5 Royal Flying Corps records of service

The records discussed in this chapter are primarily those created and held by the War Office and are concerned with service prior to the formation of the Royal Air Force on 1 April 1918.

5.1 Officers

The Royal Flying Corps was a corps of the British army and therefore officers were either commissioned into another regiment or corps and then transferred in, or they were commissioned directly into the RFC.

As with all commissioned officers of all three services, basic details about commissions and promotions can be obtained from the Army Lists. Officers of the RFC (Military Wing) and RFC appear in the Army Lists from 1912 until 1919.

Immediate pre-First World War records of service for RFC officers who left the service prior to the outbreak of the First World War do not exist. If he joined another regiment or corps prior to transfer, there is a possibility that an incomplete record of service covering an officer's initial (i.e. pre-RFC) service may be found in WO 25 or WO 76. The majority of RFC officers' records of service are to be found in the record classes WO 339 and WO 374.

5.1.1 WO 339 and WO 374

The records in these two War Office record classes are arranged in different ways. WO 339 is arranged by War Office 'Long Number' (unique identifying number) and WO 374 is arranged alphabetically.

In order to obtain the 'Long Number' for use with WO 339, it is necessary to consult the index of Officers' Long Numbers in WO 338.

WO 338 consists of 23 indexes which are available on microfilm in the Microfilm Reading Room. WO 338/1–21 consists of an alphabetical index of officers who were commissioned from 1901–20. WO 338/22 is the name index of officers commissioned between 1871 and 1901.

Each index is arranged in five columns giving: surname, forename/initial(s), regiment/corps, 'long number', rank. The regiment or corps an officer served in is indicated either by abbreviations for corps or by pre-1882 numerical regimental designator. In many cases the numerical reference may be made up to two numbers by a '/'. The first number is the battalion and the second number the regiment. Thus, 7/45 is the 7th Battalion, Notts and Derby Regiment (Sherwood Foresters). Details relating to regimental numbers can be found in the Army List.

In many cases the references found in WO 338 appear in a different form from the purely numerical. If a file reference is prefixed with a 'P', the file is still retained by the Ministry of Defence. If a file reference is prefixed by the first letter of the surname, the first vowel of the surname, and a number, the file may survive in WO 374.

Once you have obtained the 'Long Number' of the officer whose record is being sought, you need to look that number up in the WO 339 class list. The 'Long Number' is the number on the right hand side of the page, with the WO 339 piece number being on the left. If you use the on-line lists, to identify the 'Long Number' click on the 'Details' icon to show the original reference (the 'Long Number').

WO 374, which is arranged alphabetically, contains the records of service of officers commissioned into the Territorial Army, as well as many files of officers who had been commissioned prior to 1901 and who had retired before the First World War but were recalled.

5.1.2 AIR 1

Although the records in AIR 1 were deposited at the PRO by the Air Ministry, many were originally created by the RFC when it was a corps of the British Army. There are numerous files containing details about RFC officers, arranged both by unit and under general headings. Subjects include:

- Roll of officers of the RFC with the BEF, 4–30 August 1914
  AIR 1/2442/305/18/8
- Chart of Air Service Officers
  AIR 1/2530
- Posting of officers after completion of course at Central Flying School, 1913–15
  AIR 1/787/204/4/609
- Names of officers for promotion examination, July–August 1914
  AIR 1/764/204/4/225
- Nominal roll of officers, NCOs and men who proceeded to France, August 1914
  AIR 1/765/204/4/237

- Seniority roll of RFC officers, July 1914
  AIR 1/774/204/4/364

The are numerous files concerning officers' correspondence, personal reports, details relating to next of kin, etc. Most of these files are arranged under unit headings.

5.2 Airmen

Although AIR 79 contains the records of service of men of the RFC (see Section 7.3.1), the War Office did keep a number of records of service of men of the RFC who were discharged from the service before the RAF was formed. These are described in the following sections.

5.2.1 WO 97

The records of men who were discharged before the end of 1913 are in the record class WO 97. This class is arranged alphabetically. For further details about this class see Section 4.2.

5.2.2 WO 363 and WO 364

The majority of records of service of other ranks who saw service in the First World War were destroyed by enemy action (a fire at the War Office repository) in September 1940. The surviving records, arranged in two record classes (WO 363 and WO 364), are being made available on microfilm.

WO 363 contains records of men who survived the war, who were killed in action, died of wounds or disease, who were executed, or who were discharged from the service for other reasons. The records in this class, known as the 'Burnt Records', are being microfilmed with the help of a generous grant from the Heritage Lottery Fund, and as such will not be completed until 2003. At the time of writing surnames beginning with the letters A–F, N, O, Q, U, V, W, X, Y and Z are available.

The records in WO 363 may contain attestation and discharge data, details of physique, medical and conduct records, details of next of kin and details of promotions, postings and overseas service. As these records are those which survived both fire and water damage, their physical quality is very poor.

After the Second World War, the War Office put the surviving records into an alphabetical sequence and appealed to other government departments holding records relating to servicemen who had seen service in the First World War to return them to the War Office to replace the records lost in 1940. The majority of the returned records came from the Ministry of Pensions and primarily related to men who had been discharged from the army as a result of sickness or wounds contracted or received between 1914 and 1920.

Beyond the normal type of military data found in WO 97 or WO 363, the records in WO 364 contain detailed medical records relating to the reasons why an individual was discharged from the army. It is also possible find numerous records of pre-First World War pensioners who returned the colours in 1914, and who, although they did not see service overseas, did see service in the United Kingdom. Thus in WO 364 it is possible to find men of the RFC and former members of the RE Balloon Section.

5.3 Case study

Artefacts such as medals, personal papers or a memorial plaque can provide a useful starting point when researching a military career, even if the individual died in service.

5.3.1 Alan Geoffrey Fox

An end as a beginning to a research project; such is the case of A.G. Fox.

The next of kin of all those men and women who died up to seven years after the end of the First World War as a result of war service received a bronze Memorial Plaque (see Figure 4). The medal was given whether they were killed in action, died of wounds or disease or in an accident whilst on military service. Sometimes known as the 'Death Plaque' or 'Dead Man's Penny', the Memorial Plaque, which was cast in bronze, contains the name, usually in full, of the person it commemorates. Many plaques are of course identical; how many William Smiths died in the war?

A name search on the Commonwealth War Graves Commission (CWGC) website (http://www.cwgc.org) showed only one Alan Geoffrey Fox as having died during the First World War. (This search could also have been done by contacting the CWGC in writing – see Chapter 15.) The plaque for Allan Geoffrey Fox is thus unique.

The CWGC describe Fox as one of the first five officers in the army taught to fly. In the history of British military aviation Fox is obviously very important.

Alan Geoffrey Fox was born in London on 6 November 1887, son of Charles James and Beatrice Clara Fox. He was commissioned as Second Lieutenant in the Royal Engineers in February 1908.

Figure 4 Memorial Plaque for Alan Geoffrey Fox

Little is known of Fox's career before 1910. However, in the July 1914 *Army List*, he is shown as having joined the Royal Engineers Balloon School in February 1910, and being promoted to Lieutenant (Lt) in July of the same year. The creation of the Air Battalion, Royal Engineers and his transfer to it in April 1911 are also noted. The subsequent creation of the Royal Flying Corps and Fox's transfer to it on 13 May 1912 are also shown.

As Fox was one of the founding pilots of the RFC, the chance of finding documents relating to him in AIR 1 was very high. A roll of officers of the RFC from May 1912 – August 1913 in AIR 1/803/204/4/1158 shows the following:

> Lt. Temporary Captain Fox, A.G.
> Promoted Lt 30 July 1910
> Promoted Captain (Capt.) Temporary 20 October 1912
> Date of Royal Aero Club Certificate No. 176, 30 January 1912, with Special Certificate No. 5 (to fly airships) 16 July 1912 (see Figure 5.)
> Date of Gazette to Military Wing RFC 13 May 1912
> Currently employed as Flight Commander No. 3 squadron

Figure 5 Royal Aero Club Certificate
photograph of Alan Geoffrey Fox

Fox's entry on this list can be seen in Figure 6.

Just after the outbreak of the First World War, the Royal Flying Corps carried out a survey of the aircraft types its pilots could fly. Such was the ability of Fox, he was noted as being able to fly any machine (AIR 1/761/204/4/153).

Travelling to France on 29 August 1914, Fox joined the RFC Aircraft Park but returned to England in mid-September. Returning to France on 24 October 1914, this time he joined a squadron, 5 Squadron, rather than serving at the Aircraft Park. On an unknown date Fox left 5 Squadron and joined the unit, 16 Squadron, he was to serve in until his death.

The work summary of 16 Squadron, in AIR 1/1253/204/8/9, records just two flights carried out by Fox. The first flight on 3 May 1915 was a reconnaissance flight, but it was unsuccessful owing to a leaking radiator. The second and last operational flight by Alan Geoffrey Fox whilst serving with 16 Squadron was also to be his last.

Taking off in Voisin no. 1877 at 3.00 a.m. on 9 May 1915, Fox's task was to bomb a bridge over the Le Bassee-Dom canal. According to the squadron work summary, he failed to return. Interestingly there is an Aircraft Log Book (AIR 1/2070/ 204/412/1877) for the plane Fox flew on his last operational flight, and it is one of a number of sources in AIR 1 which provide details into the circumstances of his death and subsequent burial. The Aircraft Log Book notes that Fox took off with two 100 pound bombs (these would have slowed the plane down considerably) and that he was brought down between the German and French lines. The plane was burnt by bombs thrown from the German trenches. Captain Fox's body was recovered at night by the French and buried at Cambrin. Another report in AIR 1 actually records the names of the French soldiers who recovered his body (AIR 1/1254/204/8/29). So ended the life, at the age of 27, of one of the RFC's most able pilots.

Fox's records of service can be found in WO 339/7034 and AIR 76/168. His career can be further expanded upon by looking at the numerous AIR 1 references quoted in the text.

Research tip

1. The RFC was a corps of the army. Consequently records relating to men of the RFC may be found in WO as well as AIR record classes.

ROLL OF OFFI[...]

Rank	Name		Regiment	Date of Joining	Date of Promotion Lieut:	Capt:	Major	Date of R.Ae.C Certificate	Date of Passing CFS Exam; & Pilot's Cert	Date of Gazette to Mil: Wing		
BA Major	SYKES.	F.H.	15th HUSSARS		1:10:08	3:6:13		95 20/1/11		13:5:12	1414	1914
MAJOR	HIGGINS. D.S.O.	J.F.A.	R.F.A.			30:8:11	26:4 31/1/12	4:10:12		28:10:12		
Major	BROOKE POPHAM.	H.R.M.	Ox. & Bucks		4:11:04	3:6:13	108 9/7/11			13:5:12	'O' 1401	
CAPT	BURKE	C.J.	R. Irish Rgt.		22:12:09	3:6:13	260 10/10/10			18:5:12	RFRC 1401	
CAPT	CARDEN	A.D.	R. Eng		1:4:04		28A 8/1/12			13:5:12		
LIEUT	MAITLAND	E.M.	ESSEX RGT.		13:1:11		French			13:5:12		
	RALEIGH.	G.H.	-		8:1:04		146 4/3/12			13:5:12	1403	
	MUSGRAVE	H.	R. ENG		1:3:05		357 7/7/11	22:4:13	30:4:13		1404 'O'	DFRC 1401
MAJOR	BRABAZON	Hon. C.A.	IRISH GDS.		15:6:04	1912:13	279 3/1/12	4:12:12	5:12:12		1909	
	BARRINGTON-KENNETT. B.H.		GREN. GDS.				48 14/4/11		13:5:12	1909	
LIEUT		L.A.W.	WELSH RGT.		13:5:04		159 14/4/11		13:5:12	1904	
LIEUT	BEOR.	BR.W.	R. ARTY.		3:11:03		105 2/5/11			13:5:12		
	CONNER.	D.G.	R.G.		29:4:04		54 7/6/11			13:5:12	DFRC Cert. 1906	
	WATERLOW.	C.M.	R. ENG		28:12:04		Mil			18:5:12	RFRC 1906	
	REYNOLDS.	H.R.P.	-		25:6:10		92 4/4/11			13:5:12		
	BECKE.	J.H.W.	NOTTS v DERBY			28:4:09	286 9/1/12	4:10:12	28:10:12		1906	
TEMP CAPT	LONGCROFT.	C.A.H.	WELSH RGT.		13:12:06	13:8:13	122 7/3/12			13:5:12	1906	1911
CAPT	FOX.	A.G.	R. ENG		30:4:10					13:5:12		
CAPT	DAWES.	G.W.P.	R. BERKS.		30:4:11		17 26/1/10			13:5:12		
	HERBERT	P.W.L.	NOTTS v DERBY		16:2:04	21:1:13	244 7/1/11	24:10:12	13:4:13		1908	
	BEATTY.	W.O.	R. Eng's			21:12:12	89 3/7/11	14:4:13	13:5:12		
LIEUT	HYNES.	G.B.	R.G.A.		20:12:08		40 2/10/11		14:4:13		
CAPT	MELLOR	C	R. Eng			21:3:05		16:4:13	13:4:13		
	BOARD.	A.G.	S.W. Borderers		9:6:04		36 21/11/11	14:4:13	14:4:13		1902	
	McDONNELL	H.C.	R. Irish Rgt.		25:3:10		304 1/10/11	16:4:13	7:11:12		1902	
	DARBYSHIRE.	C.	4 Lanc. Fus.		22:5:11		251 24/4/11	4:12:12	7:8:13		1907	
	PIGOT.	R.	RIFLE BRIGADE		28:12:11		352 24/1/11	18:3:13	14:4:13		1906	
	TUCKER	F.H.G.	WORCESTER		22:6:12		351 24/10/11	16:4:13	28:11:12		1903	
	SHEPHARD.	G.S.	R. Fus.		5:5:04	16:1:13	215 16/5/11	28:11:12	25:8:13		
	PICTON-WARLOW.	W.	Bn. Welch			7:6:13	451 1/4/11	15:8:13	11:4:13		1906	
LIEUT	MACLEAN.	A.C.H.	R. Scots.		1:4:05		298 9/1/12	10:1:13	28:1:13		1904	
	PEPPER.	J.W.	R.G.A.		24:5:05		98 6/1/11	19:12:12			
	BOURKE	U.J.D.	Ox. & Bucks		20:4:06		409 1/3/13	15:11:13	14:8:13		1909	
	HARVEY.	E.G.	3 Wilts Rgt.		20:10:06		FR 21/2/13	16:4:13	14:4:13		1909	
	BURROUGHS.	J.E.G.	3 Wilts Rgt.		6:3:04		FR 21/2/13	16:4:13	14:4:13		1902	
	TODD.	G.E.	WELCH RGT.		9:8:04		385 7/1/13	15:8:13	25:8:13		1907	1905
	GLANVILLE.	H.F.	W. India Rgt.		6:11:04		304 1/10/11	16:4:13	14:4:13			1914
	HOLT.	F.V.	Ox. & Bucks		11:1:08		312 1/11/11	16:4:13	14:4:13		1910	
	ANDERSON	E.Y.	R. High Lders		5:2:09		48 4/4/11		25:8:13		1910	
	DAWES.	L.	2 Mx. Rgt.		6:8:08		283 24/1/11	16:4:13	14:4:13		
	HETHERINGTON	T.G.	18th HUSSARS		20:6:09		105 19/4/11		13:5:12		
	PORTER.	G.T.	R.G.A.		25:7:09		64 7/11/11		13:5:12		
	STOPFORD.	G.B.	R.F.A.		20:12:09		300 7/9/12	5:12:12	13:1:13		
	ADAMS.	P.	2 S. Lancs.		28:12:09		445 24/5/13		14:8:13		
	WALDRON	F.F.	19th HUSSARS		11:6:10		260 24/4/11	5:12:12	27:1:13		
	MARTYN.	R.B.	2 WILTSHIRE		29:5:10		FR 7/6/12	5:12:12	14:1:13		1910	
	BOYLE	Hon. J.D.	RIFLE BDE		28:8:10		353 7/1/12	16:4:13	14:4:13		1911	
	NOEL.	M.W.	Liverpool Rt				409 7/6/13	9:10:13	14:8:13		
	SMALL.	R.G.D.	LEINSTERS.		1:5:10		280 3/1/11	Nov:13	14:8:13		
	JOUBERT de la FERTE.	P.B.	R.F.A.		28:4:10		283 3/1/12	18:3:13	7:8:13		
	PLAYFAIR.	P.H.L.	R.F.A.		28:4:10		399 21/1/13	28:11:12	28:11:12		
	SHEKLETON.	A.	R.M. Fus.		5:10:10		344 7/6/13		14:8:13		
	MILLS.	R.P.			11:10:10		356 19/1/13				

Figure 6 Roll of officers of the RFC Military Wing, May 1912 to August 19[...]

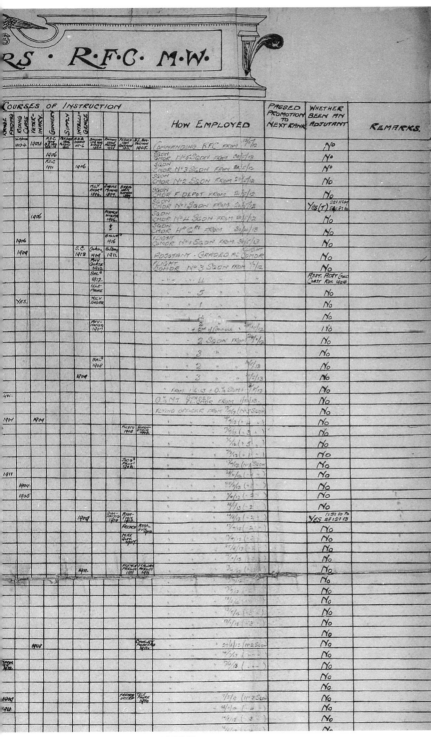

(AIR 1/803/204/4/1158)

6 Royal Naval Air Service records of service

The records of service of men of the RNAS within the ADM record classes contain details of officers and men who, for example, joined the Royal Navy and subsequently transferred into the RNAS, as well as of those who joined the Royal Naval Air Service at any time after its creation, up to 31 March 1918. The records of service of men of the RNAS who transferred into the RAF are discussed in Chapter 7.

6.1 Officers

Officers serving in the Royal Naval Air Service either transferred in from other branches of the Royal Navy or joined it directly. Thus records of service for officers of the RNAS may be found in two different record classes (ADM 196 and ADM 273), which are described in the following sections.

6.1.1 ADM 196

The records in ADM 196 consist of single sheet records of service for officers who were commissioned into the Royal Navy prior to 1908 and who subsequently specialized in aviation. The majority of the records for officers who specialized in aviation are in ADM 196/42–56, with an index in ADM 196/57. The index is not completely reliable because many of the individuals mentioned in it have no records of service. Much of ADM 196/57 has been transcribed into a card index which has converted the original index into PRO references. This card index is available in the Microfilm Reading Room.

The records of service of officers commissioned from 1908 onwards are still retained by the Ministry of Defence, and should be transferred to the PRO in the year 2000.

Records of service in ADM 196 provide date and place of birth, date of commission, the names of ships served upon, promotions, name of next of kin, details of wife and children as appropriate, and brief notes from confidential reports.

For officers promoted to the rank of Captain and above there is a further collection of records within the same class. These are arranged by date of promotion (seniority) to Captain.

ADM 196/86–94 contains the records of service of officers of the rank of Captain and above. Arranged by seniority, they cover the period 1893–1944 and therefore include records of officers who did not transfer to the RAF on its formation, and who may eventually have seen service with the Fleet Air Arm.

6.1.2 ADM 273

ADM 273 contains records of service of both commissioned and warrant officers and is comprized of the records of men who joined the RNAS after its formation in July 1914. This class consists of 30 volumes, each of which is internally indexed. There is a complete card index to this class in the Research Enquiries Room, in Card Index Island 2, drawers 135–9.

The records in this class can provide date and place of birth, date of commission and promotions, details of postings and brief notes from confidential reports.

It is possible for an officer to be found in more than one volume of ADM 273. Most of the volumes cross refer to other entries as does the index.

A number of records of service of officers who joined the RNAS after July 1914 are still retained by the Ministry of Defence and should be transferred to the PRO in the year 2000.

An example of an ADM 273 record can be seen in Figure 10 (Section 6.3.1).

6.1.3 AIR 1

As with the RFC, there are a large number of records in AIR 1 which concern RNAS officers. Most of the files concerning RNAS officers are either collected under the Admiralty section within the class, or under the records of given units. Amongst the general files are:

- List of naval officers selected for aeronautical service 1912
  AIR 1/649/17/122/400
- disposition lists of RNAS officers, showing where they were serving at a given date. These cover the period April 1914 – September 1918
  AIR 1/2108/207/49/1 – AIR 1/2110/207/49/9.

- a list of those officers of the RNAS who served in the Gallipoli campaign from April 1915 to January 1916
  AIR 1/675/21/13/1563
- Weekly return of officers and ratings at RNAS station Roehampton and Kite balloon sections abroad 1917
  AIR 1/447/15/303/40

6.2 Ratings

Although the main collection of records of service for RN ratings is ADM 188, details concerning men of the RNAS Armoured Car Units can also be found elsewhere.

6.2.1 ADM 188

The record class ADM 188 contains the records of service of all naval ratings who served at any time between 1873 and 1923. This class holds the records of men whose service encompassed the year 1873, when this particular series of records started, right up to men who enlisted in 1923. The Royal Navy changed its record keeping again in 1929 and therefore the records of men who saw service after 1928 contain little further detail beyond noting the date on which they qualified for their Long Service and Good Conduct Medals (see Section 10.5.2) or the date of death if they were a Second World War casualty.

The Royal Navy changed its service number format twice between 1873 and 1914. Between 1873 and 1893, service numbers were allocated on a 'through the door' basis; each man being given a number as he joined the service. Between 1894 and 1907, batches of numbers representing specific branches of the service were used. Therefore, men joining the Seamen and Communication branch were given numbers within a certain range and men joining the Stokers branch were given a number in a different range. All of the service numbers between 1873 and 1907 are in one sequence from 40 001 to 366 450.

In 1908 a new service numbering system was started with all branches of the services beginning again at 1, but this time the branches of the service were given different alphabetical prefixes to identify them. Therefore men joining from 1908 into the Seamen branch had service numbers prefixed with the letter 'J' and men joining the Stoker branch had service numbers prefixed with the letter 'K'.

With the creation of the Royal Naval Air Service in July 1914, the Royal Navy started a new series of service numbers for ratings joining the new service. This was prefixed with an 'F'. Many men already serving in the Royal Navy transferred into the RNAS and kept their original service numbers and it is therefore possible to find men of the RNAS with both numerical service numbers and service numbers with alphabetical prefixes.

The range of indexes available is:

ADM 188 A–Z Indexes

- Men serving in 1873 or who enlisted between then and 1891
  ADM 188/245–267
- Enlistments, 1892–1912
  ADM 188/1132–1154
- Enlistments, 1913–1923
  ADM 188/1155–1177

ADM 188 Records of Service (specifically RNAS)

- service numbers F1–F55000
  ADM 188/560–646

6.2.2 AIR 1

Although there are numerous files in AIR 1 concerning RNAS officers, there are very few which specifically concern RNAS ratings alone. Most files which mention RNAS ratings are to be found under unit records.

6.2.3 ADM 116

Although the records in ADM 116 cover a wide variety of subjects, the class is not primarily concerned with records of service. However, two files about RNAS ratings who were members of the RNAS Armoured Car section in Russia can be found in ADM 116/1625 and 1717. Details relating to such subjects as individuals' discipline and awards received, not readily available in other files, together with information contained in ADM 188, can be found here.

6.3 Case study

Family photographs (Figure 7) can provide lots of useful information about individuals, even if you have only their names. See Chapter 14 for further details about photographs.

Figure 7 Petty Officer (Mechanic)
Arthur Bedward Spencer, RNAS Armoured Cars

6.3.1 Arthur Bedward Spencer

A.B. Spencer was one of the many young men who answered his country's call for volunteers at the outbreak of the First World War. As the photograph of A.B. Spencer clearly showed him in the uniform of Petty Officer of the RNAS Armoured Car Section, the logical place to start was the name index to RN ratings in ADM 188. An entry in ADM 188/1174 showed an Arthur B. Spencer with an RNAS service number of F1769. Service number F1769 is to be found in ADM 188/563. See Figure 8.

Born in Old Basford, Nottingham, on 15 April 1891, Arthur Spencer volunteered for service as a Petty Officer Mechanic in the Royal Naval Air Service on 9 November 1914. His engagement papers (held by the Fleet Air Arm Museum) describe him as 5' 11½" tall, with auburn hair, grey eyes and a fresh complexion. His occupation on enlistment was given as hosiery manufacturer.

Further details, contained in ADM 188/563, show that after basic military training Spencer was posted to an RNAS Armoured Car Unit and it was with this unit that he was to see his initial operational service. Although no annotation was made on his

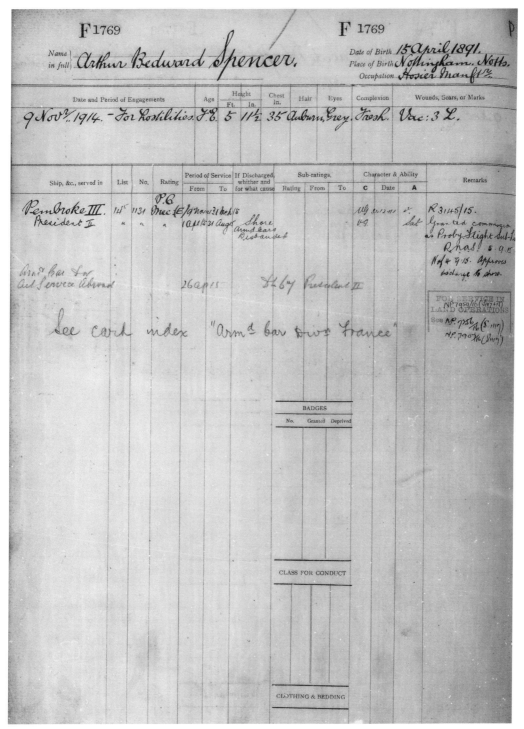

Figure 8 Naval ratings record of service for Arthur Bedward Spencer (ADM 188/563)

Figure 9 Royal Aero Club Certificate
photograph of Arthur Bedward Spencer

ADM 188 record, consultation of the medal roll in ADM 171/115 showed that he qualified for a 1914/15 Star, British War Medal and Victory Medal. However, the 'How Disposed of Column' is blank with a note to 'see officers roll'. This note indicates that at some stage in the war, Spencer was commissioned from the ranks.

Further consultation of his ADM 188 record showed a faint note stating that PO(M) A.B. Spencer was commissioned as a Probationary Flight Sub Lieutenant (FSL) on 5 September 1915. This was confirmed by looking at the Navy List.

The records of service of RNAS officers in ADM 273 show three different entries for the trainee pilot: ADM 273/7 ff74, ADM 273/23 ff211, and ADM 273/30 ff133. The first of these three entries notes that he joined the RNAS school at Eastchurch on 20 September 1915, and after a period of instruction was awarded Royal Aero Club Certificate 1903, on 16 October 1915 (see Figure 9).

After basic flying training, a posting to the RNAS air station at Killingholme with effect from 20 October 1915 for further flying instruction was to result in an unfortunate end to what appeared to have been a promising flying career.

Confidential reports in ADM 273/7 dated 20 December 1915 (Figure 10) record that Arthur Spencer lost his flying nerve. Although described as 'a good officer so far as he has gone and has been one of the best pupils', Spencer's flying days were over.

Royal Navy Aircraft Serials and Units 1911–1919 by Ray Sturtivant and Gordon Page has a very useful index of names of individuals associated with RNAS aircraft. Interestingly an entry for FSL A.B. Spencer, notes that whilst he was flying BE2C, serial number 1137, with Flight Lieutenant J.C. Brook, from Killingholme, the plane nose-dived into the Humber. Considering the date of the accident and the content of the confidential reports in ADM 273/7, it appears that this accident was the most likely cause of Spencer's loss of flying nerve.

Obviously a man of ability, FSL Spencer then spent a short period at sea aboard HMS *Penelope* before taking up a commission in the RNVR as an armaments officer, still serving with, rather than in, the RNAS.

With effect from 24 January 1916, Sub Lieutenant A.B. Spencer RNVR served as an armaments officer at a variety of RNAS air stations. Although technically an officer of the RNVR, Spencer's confidential reports were still completed by RNAS officers. All of the reports state that he was a good officer, hardworking and trustworthy, and recommended for promotion.

Eventually promoted to Lieutenant RNVR, Arthur Spencer was one of the many naval officers connected with aviation who transferred to the fledgling RAF on 1 April 1918. Not surprisingly his name appears in the first *Air Force List* in April 1918. His RAF record of service in AIR 76/477 (Figure 11) notes that after continuing his duties at Cattewater in Plymouth until after the armistice, he was eventually placed on the RAF unemployed list and retired from the RAF as Captain in July 1919.

Arthur Bedward Spencer died in 1938.

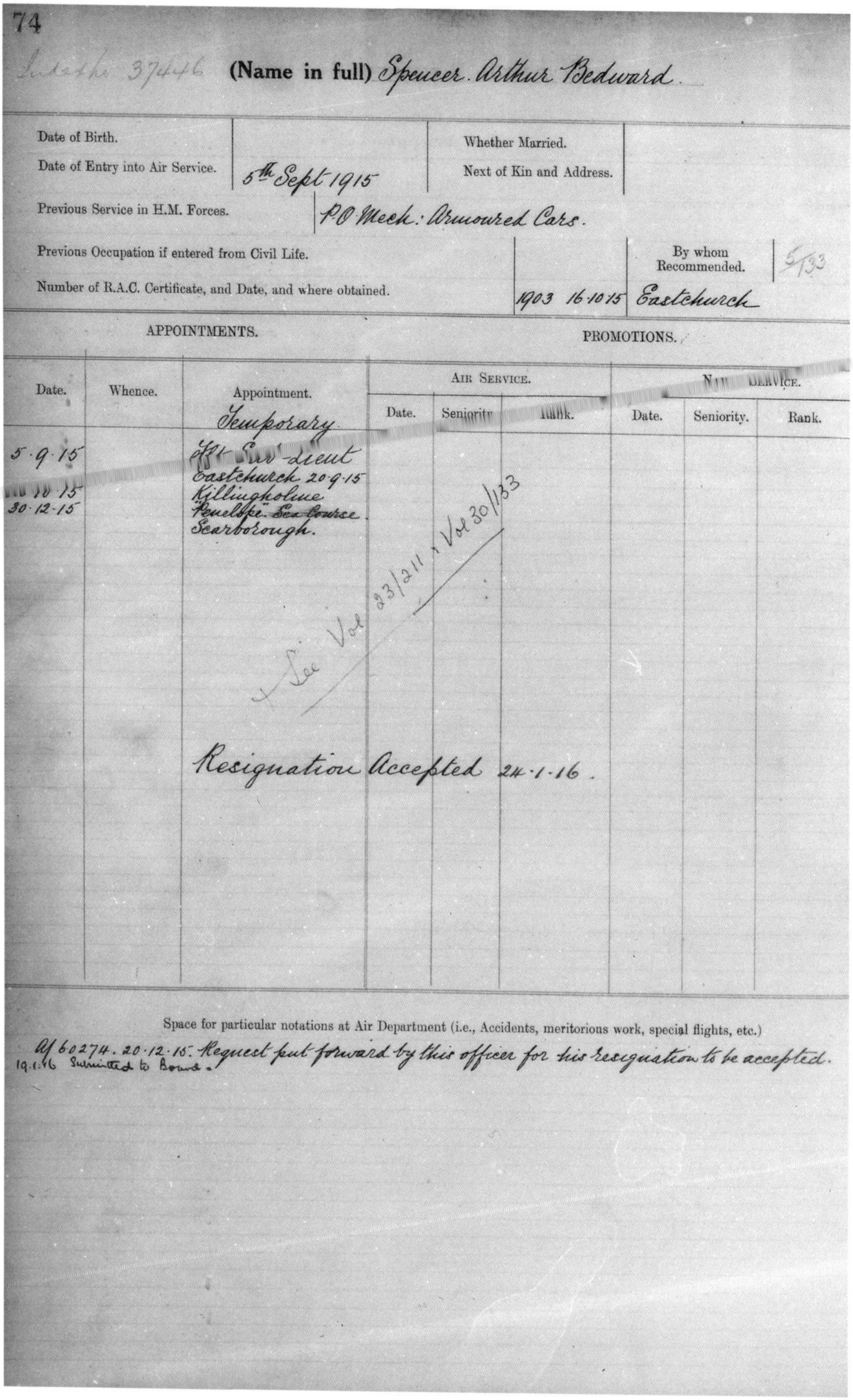

Figure 10 RNAS record of service of Arthur Bedward Spencer (ADM 273/7)

74

C<small>ONFIDENTIAL</small> R<small>EPORTS</small>.

Occasion.	Date.	By whom.	Conduct.	Ability.	Special Ability.	Languages etc.	REMARKS.
A/59980	20·12·15	Killingholme					Has made several solo flights on Caudrons & Curtiss machines, but has completely lost his nerve, & is going to tender his resignation.
A/60274	20·12·15	''					For over a month he has lost his flying nerve. Everything has been done to help him, but without success. I have watched him trying, & I consider it dangerous to allow him to go up in the air again. He has shown himself a good officer so far as he has gone, & has been quite one of the best pupils, & has a fair engineering knowledge. Wing Com.dr H. D. Briggs.
''	24·12·15	D.A.S.					Wing Com.dr Briggs asked to report whether he considers this officer suitable for the Rank of Sub-Lt R.N.A.V.R. for "E" duties, & whether if it was decided to give him this rank, he would be willing to accept it.
	4·1·16	Killingholme					Gone for a short sea course.

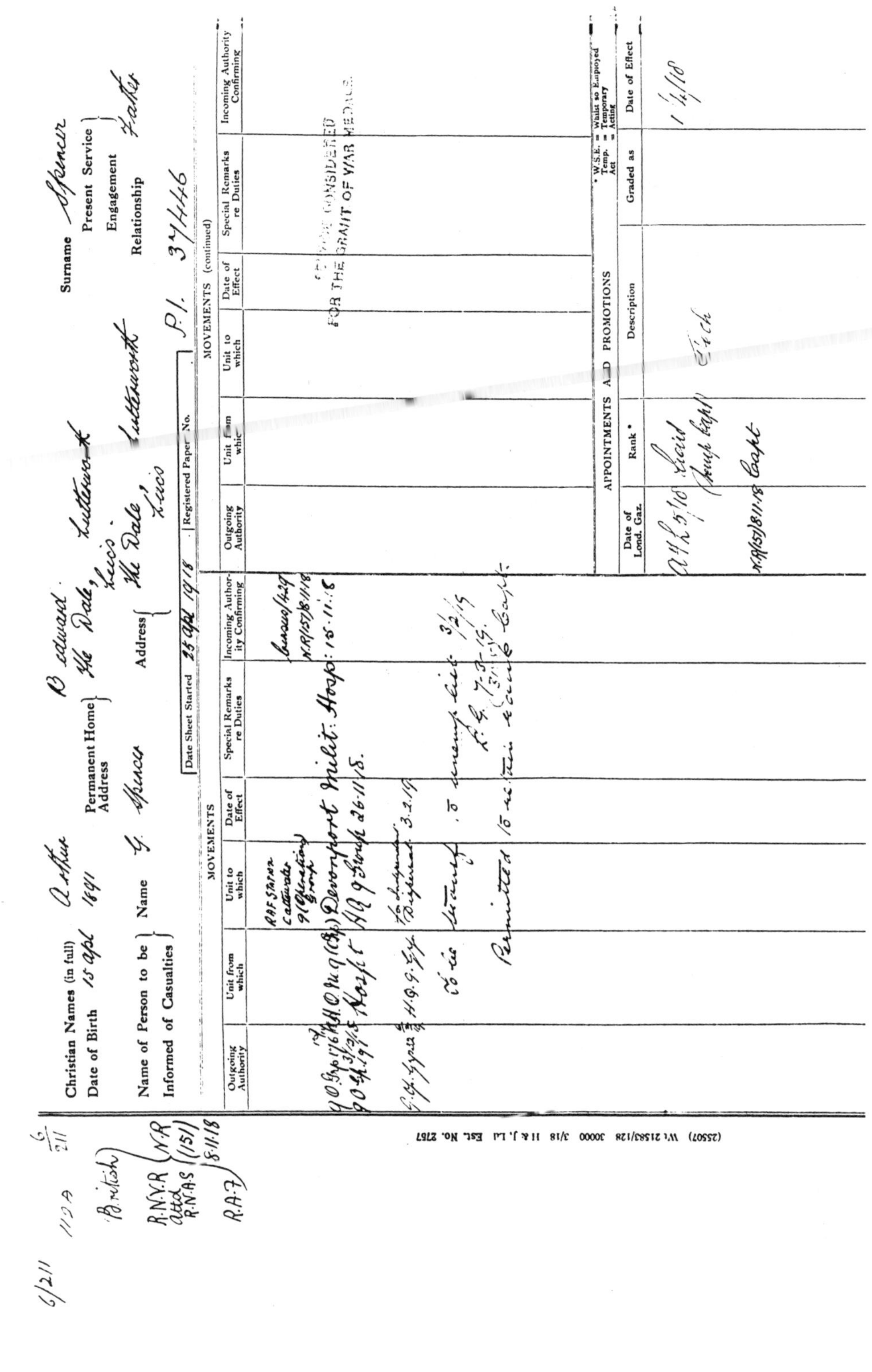

Figure 11 RAF record of service of Arthur Bedward Spencer (AIR 76/477)

7 Royal Air Force and Women's Royal Air Force records of service

7.1 Introduction

Although many of the records of service of RAF personnel were created before the formation of the RAF, in this chapter only records of service created after 31 March 1918 or which were administered by the Air Ministry, i.e. records in the AIR record classes, will be discussed.

The formal creation of the RAF on 1 April 1918 established a service which by the armistice had 27 333 officers and 263 837 other ranks. As the manpower for the new service came from the Admiralty and War Office, the Air Ministry had to set about acquiring or creating records relating to the manpower it had just inherited.

7.2 Officers

Records of service concerning RAF officers fall into two generic groups: records of service in one collection; and records which contain details relating to officers' services. The other key source concerning RAF officers, especially those who saw service after 1919, is the Air Force List.

The first *Air Force List* appeared in April 1918 and listed all of those officers who joined the new service upon its creation. Interestingly the ranks used in the early Air Force Lists are both naval and military. RAF ranks as used today did not appear until April 1919.

From April 1920 until March 1939 the Air Force List contains quite detailed information about the location and names of officers in given units. Retired Lists first appeared in the spring of 1949. The Retired Lists provide date of birth, qualifications and honours and awards, date of first commission, date of retirement and the date of the commission of the highest rank attained.

7.2.1 AIR 76

The record class AIR 76, which is available only on microfilm, comprises 567 reels of microfilm containing the records of service of most of the early officers of the RAF. The record class, which is arranged alphabetically, contains records of service of some 26 000 officers of the RAF whose service ended before the end of 1919. Records of service for officers who served after this date are still held by the Ministry of Defence.

The records in AIR 76 consist of microfilm copies of single sheet records of service, completed in many cases on both sides, which contain all of the most useful but basic information about an RAF officer. Information in an AIR 76 record includes:

- Christian name in full and surname
- date of birth
- permanent home address
- details of next of kin
- units in which an individual served and when
- appointments and promotions (with *London Gazette* dates)
- honours and awards (with *London Gazette* dates)
- medical boards.

Most of the records also note the date on which they were started and in which unit an individual was commissioned, if not directly into the RFC or RAF.

It is interesting to note that AIR 76 contains records of service of many RFC officers who lost their lives prior to the formation of the RAF.

7.2.2 AIR 1

There are numerous files in AIR 1 which contain details relating to RAF officers, both general files and files specific to given units. The wide variety of files includes many which cover both the RFC period and the RAF period from 1 April 1918 onwards. Included are files on:

- officers' flying times
- appointments and postings
- nominal rolls
- lists of prisoners of war
- dispositions of officers.

Of these files some relate to officers who of course stayed in the RAF after 1919 and for whom there is no record in AIR 76. Some of the most important of these files include:

- Nominal roll of officers recommended for permanent commissions: RAF
  May–August 1918
  AIR 1/1161/204/5/2516
- Nominal roll of officers recommended for permanent commissions: RAF
  August–September 1919
  AIR 1/1161/204/5/2517
- Nominal roll of officers granted permanent commissions: RAF
  August–September 1919
  AIR 1/1161/204/5/2518
- Permanent commissions for officers seconded from the Army to the RAF
  August–September 1919
  AIR 1/1161/204/5/2520
- Nominal rolls of officers who refused or accepted RAF commissions
  August–September 1919
  AIR 1/1161/204/5/2521

Other files of note include:

- Nominal roll of South African officers serving with the RAF
  December 1918
  AIR 1/2418/305/7
- Reports on Canadian officers with the RAF, in the field
  June–December 1918
  AIR 1/1035/204/5/1452

7.3 Airmen

There are a number of different sources where details about RAF airmen can be found, in collections of service papers in one record class (AIR 79), as well as details distributed amongst the squadron records in AIR 1. The single most important source concerning RAF other ranks, on formation of the service, is the RAF muster. This muster lists by service number all of those men who were on the strength of the new service when it was formed. Beyond name and service number, the muster gives date of enlistment into the services, trade, period of engagement and rate of pay. The RAF muster can be found in AIR 1/819/204/4/1316.

7.3.1 AIR 79

To search these records you need to know the service number of the individual you seek. See 7.3.2.

The records of service of RAF airmen with service numbers up to 329 000 are in the record class AIR 79. This record class is arranged in service number order and although it contains the records of men whose service numbers go up to 329 000, the records of many men whose service numbers lie within this range but who saw service in the Second World War are not in this record class but are retained by the Ministry of Defence.

As AIR 79 contains records up to service number 329 000, it therefore holds the records of men who formerly served in the RE Balloon Section, the Royal Flying Corps, the Royal Naval Air Service and those who entered directly into the RAF. The records are arranged as follows:

References	Service numbers
AIR 79/1–2805	RAF service numbers 1–329 000
AIR 79/2806	South African Air Corps service numbers Σ2–Σ592
AIR 79/2807	RAF Special Reservist service numbers SR1–SR25

As each piece of AIR 79 only covers a given range of service numbers it is necessary to obtain the correct service number from AIR 78, if it is not known already.

Although the RAF service numbers are in a logical numerical sequence, they do not necessarily represent a chronological sequence of enlistments. The lowest numbers represent those men who joined the RFC on formation and the highest numbers those men who joined the RAF in the immediate post-First World War period. Service numbers between 200 001 and 255 600 represent former members of the RNAS with RN service numbers F1–F55600. Service numbers 313 000–315 000 represent men who originally joined the Royal Navy prior to July 1914 and who subsequently joined the RNAS but retained their original RN service numbers until they joined the RAF.

As the service origin of men whose records can be found in AIR 79 includes all three services, so a physical variety of the different types of records, all containing similar sorts of information, may be found. Army Forms for men of the RE Balloon and RAF Forms 175 are common examples of what may be found. The RAF used examples of both naval and army forms to keep records on their personnel.

Details found in AIR 79 include the usual physical description, date and place of birth data, together with enlistment and discharge dates. Depending on the type of record held in AIR 79 the type and amount of information may then vary. In most cases if a man joined the RAF from the RNAS or Army, then the relevant dates will be annotated on his RAF record. Most RAF records are on an RAF Form 175 and as such contain the following details:

- date and place of birth
- physical description
- dates of attestation and discharge
- cause of discharge
- dates of promotions
- postings
- details of next of kin (wife and children as applicable)
- medical and disciplinary history
- details of medals.

7.3.2 AIR 78

A nominal index of both RAF airmen and WRAF women is available on microfilm in the Microfilm Reading Room. The index, which is of variable quality, provides the surname and first name or initial(s) and the service number, which you need to use AIR 79. Once you have the service number of the airman you seek, apply that number to the AIR 79 class list and order the piece of AIR 79 which encompasses that service number. (For women, see below.)

7.3.3 AIR 1

There are numerous files within AIR 1 which contain details about RAF airmen, but once again they are dispersed amongst the various units' records, rather than in a specific section. If you know a unit in which an individual served, try a keyword search on the 'On-line Lists'.

7.4 Women's Royal Air Force

No records of service of officers of the WRAF have survived.

The surviving records of service of other rank members of the WRAF are in the record class AIR 80. This class is arranged alphabetically and therefore no service number is needed to search it. In most cases there is only a single record sheet giving details about each woman. These record sheets vary and with them the type and amount of information given about each individual. They all give a physical description of the individuals concerned, and details of how and where they were employed. The most unusual terms to be found on these records of service are 'Mobile' and 'Immobile'. Mobile members of the WRAF were full time members of the service who lived on the camp where they worked or in lodgings nearby, and who were therefore able to be posted anywhere. Immobile members of the WRAF were part time staff who lived at home.

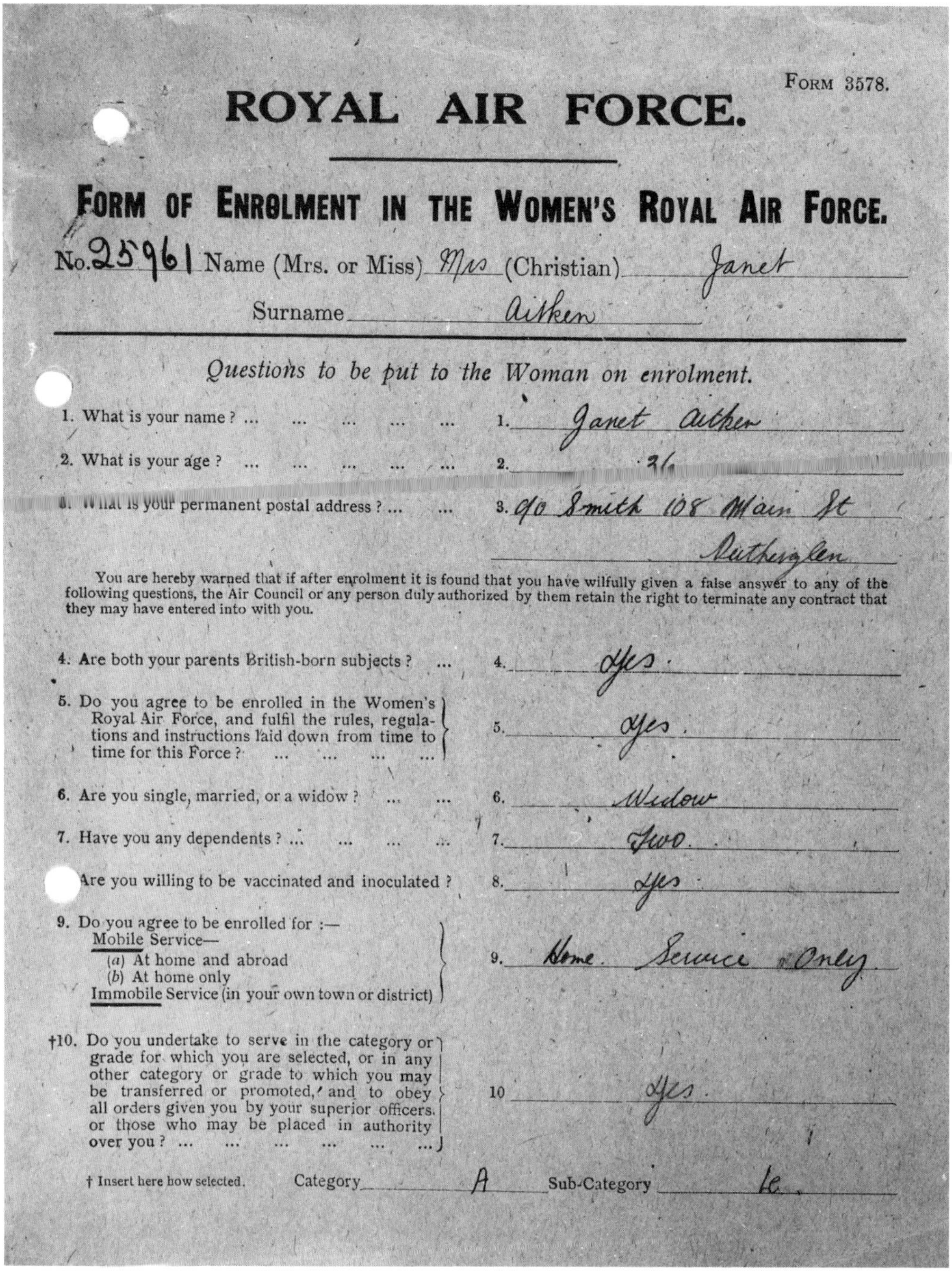

FORM 3578.

ROYAL AIR FORCE.

FORM OF ENROLMENT IN THE WOMEN'S ROYAL AIR FORCE.

No. 25961 Name (Mrs. or Miss) Mrs (Christian) Janet

Surname Aitken

Questions to be put to the Woman on enrolment.

1. What is your name? ... 1. Janet Aitken
2. What is your age? ... 2. 26
3. What is your permanent postal address? ... 3. c/o Smith 108 Main St Rutherglen

You are hereby warned that if after enrolment it is found that you have wilfully given a false answer to any of the following questions, the Air Council or any person duly authorized by them retain the right to terminate any contract that they may have entered into with you.

4. Are both your parents British-born subjects? ... 4. Yes.
5. Do you agree to be enrolled in the Women's Royal Air Force, and fulfil the rules, regulations and instructions laid down from time to time for this Force? ... 5. Yes.
6. Are you single, married, or a widow? ... 6. Widow
7. Have you any dependents? ... 7. Two.
8. Are you willing to be vaccinated and inoculated? 8. Yes
9. Do you agree to be enrolled for :— Mobile Service— (*a*) At home and abroad (*b*) At home only Immobile Service (in your own town or district) 9. Home. Service Only.

†10. Do you undertake to serve in the category or grade for which you are selected, or in any other category or grade to which you may be transferred or promoted, and to obey all orders given you by your superior officers, or those who may be placed in authority over you? ... 10 Yes.

† Insert here how selected. Category A Sub-Category le.

Figure 12 Typical WRAF record of service (AIR 80/2)

The records of service are usually found on either Army Form B103 or RAF Form 3677 Z, both of which contain details of length of service and trade. An example of an AIR 80 record can be see in Figure 12.

7.5 Case study

7.5.1 Ernest Albert Hogg

Ernest Albert Hogg initially volunteered to serve in the army, under the 'Derby Scheme', in December 1915. His chosen regiment was the 20 Battalion, King's Royal Rifle Corps. When he was called up for service in May 1916, instead of joining his chosen regiment, he opted to transfer into the Royal Flying Corps.

On mobilization, Hogg, allocated the RFC service number 103993, was described as 5′ 7″ tall, with dark hair, blue eyes and a fresh complexion. Born in Bermondsey, south London on 16 September 1894, Ernest Hogg was to spend the next 4 years at various RFC and latterly RAF units, in both the United Kingdom and France. As he had been an electrical fitter in civilian life, it was not surprising to find him graded as an Air Fitter shortly after some basic RFC training.

Hogg's first operational service overseas was with No. 2 Aircraft Depot in France between 23 August and 3 September 1917. A short introduction to active service was ended when he became ill with, as far as his record is concerned, an unknown ailment.

Returning to France in February 1918, Hogg was to serve there until September 1919. Finally being demobilized in April 1920, it appears that Hogg resumed his pre-war trade. However, with the emerging German threat of the late 1930s, he joined the RAF Reserve on 17 July 1939. What became of him after that date is at present unknown.

Ernest Hogg's record of service can be found in AIR 79/936 and it is illustrated in Figure 13.

Research tips

1. Use the Army and Air Force Lists to obtain basic data on RFC and RAF officers.

2. RAF airmen's records of service are arranged by service number. You need to know what numbers to look for when you use AIR 79.

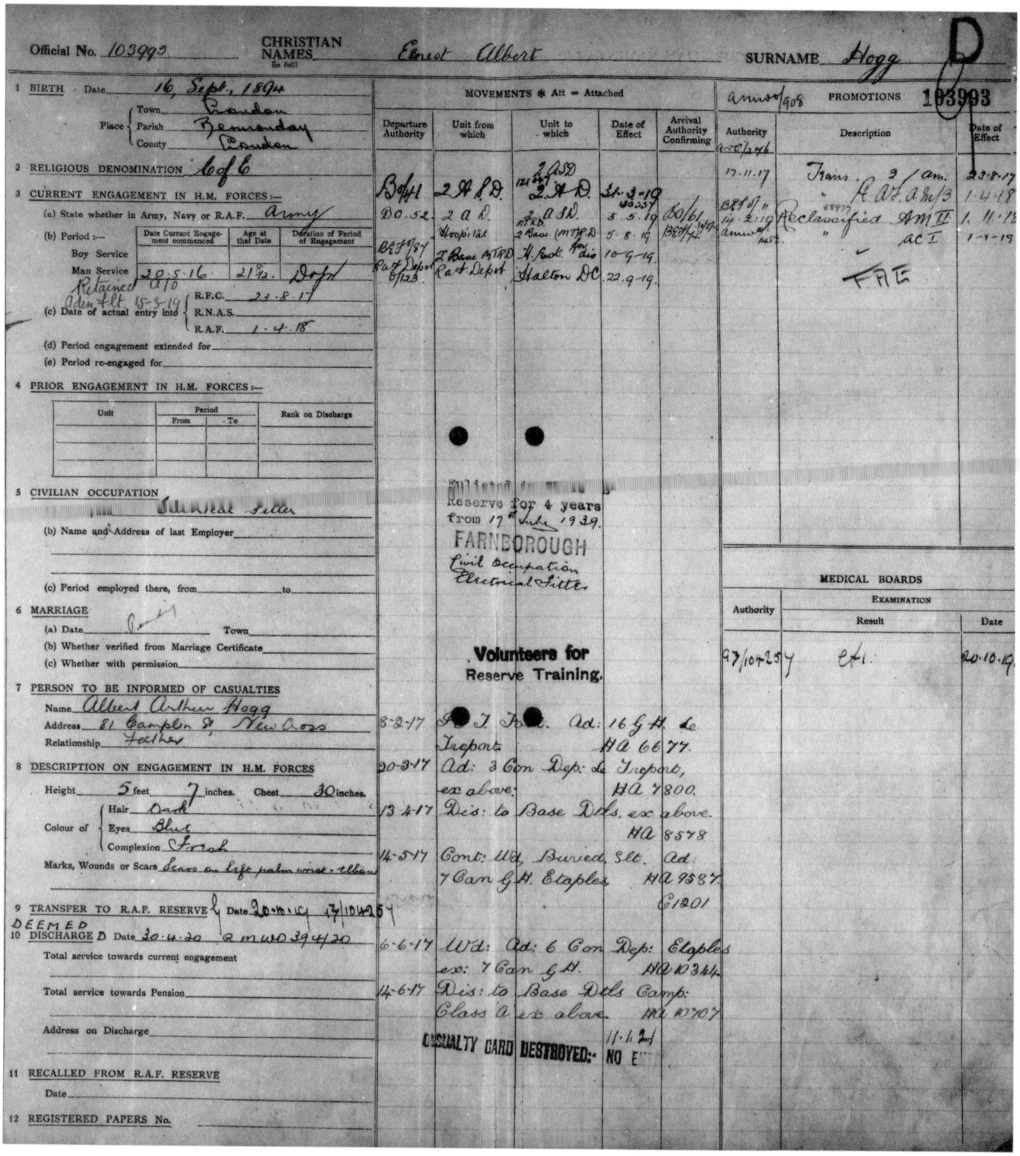

Official No. 103993 CHRISTIAN NAMES (in full) Ernest Albert SURNAME Hogg

1 BIRTH Date 16, Sept, 1894
Place: Town London; Parish Bermondsey; County London

2 RELIGIOUS DENOMINATION C of E

3 CURRENT ENGAGEMENT IN H.M. FORCES:—
(a) State whether in Army, Navy or R.A.F. Army
(b) Period:— Boy Service; Man Service 20.5.16 | 21 | D of W
Retained A/O
(c) Date of actual entry into R.F.C. 23.8.17; R.N.A.S.; R.A.F. 1.4.18
(d) Period engagement extended for
(e) Period re-engaged for

4 PRIOR ENGAGEMENT IN H.M. FORCES:—

Unit	Period From	Period To	Rank on Discharge

5 CIVILIAN OCCUPATION Electrical Fitter
(b) Name and Address of last Employer
(c) Period employed there, from to

6 MARRIAGE
(a) Date Town
(b) Whether verified from Marriage Certificate
(c) Whether with permission

7 PERSON TO BE INFORMED OF CASUALTIES
Name Albert Arthur Hogg
Address 81 Camplin St, New Cross
Relationship Father

8 DESCRIPTION ON ENGAGEMENT IN H.M. FORCES
Height 5 feet 7 inches. Chest 30 inches.
Colour of Hair Dark; Eyes Blue; Complexion Fresh
Marks, Wounds or Scars Scars on left palm wrist, elbow

9 TRANSFER TO R.A.F. RESERVE Date 20.10.19 17/10425
10 DEEMED DISCHARGE D Date 30.4.20 2 MWO 394/20
Total service towards current engagement
Total service towards Pension
Address on Discharge

11 RECALLED FROM R.A.F. RESERVE Date

12 REGISTERED PAPERS No.

MOVEMENTS * Att = Attached

Departure Authority	Unit from which	Unit to which	Date of Effect	Arrival Authority Confirming
B of 1	2 A.S.D.	2 A.S.D.	31.3.19	
DO.52	2 A.D.	2 A.D.	5.5.19	DO/61
	Hospital	2 Base (MTRD)	5.8.19	
BEF/87	2 Base MTRD	H. Fort. for dis	10.9.19	
Rat Depot 6/123	Rat Depot	Halton DC	22.9.19	

Enlisted ... Reserve for 4 years from 17th July 1939. FARNBOROUGH. Civil Occupation Electrical Fitter

Volunteers for Reserve Training.

8-2-17 R.F.C. Ad: 16 G.H. Le Treport HA 6677.
20-3-17 Ad: 3 Con Dep: Le Treport, ex above. HA 7800.
13-4-17 Dis: to Base Dets, ex above. HA 8578
14-5-17 Cont: Wd, Buried, Slt. Ad: 7 Can G.H. Etaples HA 9587 C/201
6-6-17 Wd: Ad: 6 Con Dep: Etaples ex: 7 Can G.H. HA 10344
14-6-17 Dis: to Base Dets Camp: Class A ex above. HA 10707

CASUALTY CARD DESTROYED: 11.1.21 NO E...

PROMOTIONS 103993

Authority	Description	Date of Effect
17.11.17	Trans. 2/Am.	23.8.17
	R.A.F. AM/3	1.4.18
BE 18/1	Reclassified AM II	1.11.18
14.2.19	AC I	1.1.19

MEDICAL BOARDS

Authority	Examination Result	Date
97/10425	C1	20.10.19

Figure 13 RAF record of service of Ernest Albert Hogg (AIR 79/936)

8 Operational records

8.1 Royal Engineers Balloon Section

As there were so few military operations in which the Royal Engineers Balloon Sections were involved, the records relating to these operations are few.

A general report relating to balloons, covering the period 1885–6, which covers the first major use of balloons in Bechuanaland and the Sudan, can be found in WO 32/6067 (Code 45(N)). A report from the Officer Commanding Royal Engineers in Bechuanaland in 1885 can be found in WO 32/8204 (Code O(AU)). Further reports relating to British Army operations in the same region can be found in WO 33/44 (Figure 14) and 45, WO 106/264, 6242 and 6243 and WO 147/29 and 35.

Nos 1–3 Balloon Sections, Royal Engineers, were involved in the Boer War. A summary of the Role of the Royal Engineers in the Boer War can be found in WO 108/283–298.

A report of the employment of No 4. Balloon Section, Royal Engineers in China, 1900–1902, can be found in WO 32/6059 (Code O(J)).

8.2 Royal Flying Corps

Operational records for brigades, wings, squadrons and miscellaneous units of the Royal Flying Corps can be found in AIR 1. Whether the unit is a brigade, wing or squadron, as long as the number or name of that unit is known, then the operational records of that unit can be found.

Many different types of operational records exist in AIR 1, not only squadron record books and summaries of work but also reports of activities, combat reports, hours flown, particulars of officers and numerous photographs.

Most of the operational records contain such data as what the task was, who was involved, when the operation took place and what the outcome was. To create a full picture of a particular operation or incident it may be necessary to consult a number of sources. By using operational records from each part of the chain of command, from

97

706

observing elevation, by aid of the long guy-rope and pilot line manned by gangs of men below, right through the intricate windings of the Kaffir village, and out on to the high ground to the south of the village. Here the General Officer Commanding descended, and the balloon was safely conveyed back again and bagged down securely for the night. This days operations were very successful throughout.

It being very desirable to test practically the condition and capabilities of 8th April each of the balloons in turn, it was decided to fill the "Spy" 7,000 feet this day.

Work was commenced at 6.30 a.m. The "Spy" being a bran new balloon barely completed at Chatham in time to be packed up and put on board ship for this Expedition, it was a somewhat doubtful and anxious question as to how far she would prove to be damaged, or stuck together in her folds, by the long confinement and great heat to which all the balloons were necessarily exposed. She proved to be a little stuck together in her folds in places, but not seriously so. The balloon was full about 11 a.m. Major Elsdale reported to the Commanding Royal Engineer and General Officer Commanding, and received instructions to march out towards Rooi Grond which the General was then proceeding. Start about 12.15 p.m. with the long guy-rope and two guiding ropes on and got her through the Kaffir village in safety. The wind was blowing pretty fresh from the N.W., the general direction of the route being E. The balloon was let up about 1,000 feet on the long guy-rope, which was made fast to the mule wagon. The whole of the necessary detachment for working the balloon then got on to the wagon, and trotted out about 6 miles on the Rooi Grond road. The balloon rode easily and quietly at this great elevation above the ground, and could readily have been conveyed thus all the way to Rooi Grond or beyond if required. The wagon was then halted and Major Elsdale made an ascent, having first hauled the balloon down by aid of a running snatch-block, and a towing party to haul it along the guy-rope.

The General Officer Commanding left Mafeking about 1 p.m., and riding fast overtook the balloon about 2 p.m. Major Elsdale then made an ascent with the wind very fresh, much too strong and gusty to admit of any favourable or deliberate observation.

Tried the telephone communication with the ground below, but found that in this wind the telephones would not work on account of the vibration and oscillation, of balloon and ropes. Major Elsdale then descended to report to the General, letting the balloon up again some hundreds of feet for security from the ground currents. She, however, tore off her neck loop in a violent gust of wind and started a rent in the envelope. To prevent further damage to the balloon, she was then emptied and got in.

The sappers repaired the damage done, in the intervals of work with other balloons on the two or three following days. She was then ready for duty again, and was refilled when required in the following week.

This new balloon was found to be an excellent one, and holding the gas remarkably well. The general result of this day's experience goes to show that it is quite possible should the exigencies of service require it, to convey balloons long distances, and work them for observation, under more or less disadvantageous conditions for observation, in windy and unfavourable weather, but with a considerably increased risk of accidents, whether to the balloons and gear, or to the officers employed in making the ascent.

Next morning commenced filling the "Feo," 4,500 feet, at 9.30 a.m., and 9th April. finished at 11.30 a.m. The weather was windy and unfavourable. The Commanding Royal Engineer was away from Mafeking, so in the absence of orders she was kept bagged down all day.

Commenced work at 6 a.m. Filled up the "Feo," which had shrunk from 10th April. condensation of the gas due to change of temperature during the night (the nights being cold in these elevated regions); we also inflated the two 370-feet pilot balloons, as satellites for the "Feo" to assist her lift. Reported to the General Officer Commanding, who came to inspect the balloons about 7 a.m. Major Elsdale then made an ascent with one satellite attached, and the

(517)   2 c

Figure 14 RE Balloon Section mentioned in the Bechuanaland operational report (WO 33/44)

the unit the man was serving in at the time upwards, a more informative account of a given incident can be created.

Beyond the records in AIR 1, it is also possible to find general reports of RFC activities in WO 158.

Records of a number of squadrons are also in AIR 1. These records can be found by using the squadron number as the keyword when searching the 'On-line Lists'. They usually provide overall statistics concerning unit performance, awards and kills, together with a brief history of the unit. These histories can also be found by using the unit index in the AIR 1 class list.

A typical example of an RFC squadron operational record, in this case a 16 Squadron, RFC, Work Summary (AIR 1/1253/204/8/9), can be seen in Figure 15.

8.3 Royal Naval Air Service

Although the RNAS was the responsibility of the Admiralty prior to the formation of the RAF in April 1918, the majority of operational records concerning RNAS squadrons are in AIR 1. As with the RFC squadron records, as long as the number of the squadron is known, the records can easily be found in AIR 1.

The majority of Admiralty records concerning RNAS activities can be found in ADM 137. There are two ways of identifying records in this class. One is to use the ADM 137 lists to identify relevant Admiralty Historical Section records in the record class. The other is to use the Admiralty Index and Digest in ADM 12 to identify original Admiralty file references and then convert them into ADM 137 file references. Beyond using the ADM 12 alphabetical sections to obtain references concerning awards granted to individuals, Digest (Subject) codes 3 (Actions with The Enemy) and 90 (Aviation) will provide the most useful items. Original files referred to in ADM 12 may be found in ADM 1, ADM 116 and ADM 137.

A guide, 'How to Use ADM 12', is available upon request from the Research Enquiries Room desk.

Operational records of a number of RNAS airship units based in the west of England can be found in the Plymouth Station records in ADM 131/64.

R.F.C. Form No. 302.

SUMMARY OF WORK.

No.16 Squadron, Royal Flying Corps.   Date 9th May. 1915

Type	Pilot	Observer	Duty	Hour of Departure	Hour of Return	Remarks
B.E2c. 1752	2/Lt.Walker	Lt.James.	Attempted Reconnaissance	4.am	4.20am	Unsuccessful owing to strong wind.
-:-	-:-	Capt.Cairnes	Reconnaissance	12.35pm	2.5.pm	1.Copy of report to 1st Army, 2 copies to 1st Advanced Wing.
BE2c. 588	t.Cunningham.	Lieut.James	Reconnaissance.	6.50am	8.25am	1.copy of report to 1st Army, 2 copies to 1st Advanced Wing.
Voisin 1877	Capt.Fox.	Nil	Bomb dropping as ordered	3.am		Did not return.
-:- 1879	Lt.Glanville.	Nil	Bomb Dropping as ordered	3.am	4.45am	Bombs dropped. (Pilot wounded during journey.)
-:- 1879	Lt.Braithwaite.	Nil	Testing Machine.	3.45pm	4.0pm	Satisfactory.
-:- 1868	Lt.Eworll.	Lt.Seaford.	Reconnaissance.	3.50am		Have not yet returned.
MF. 1853	Capt.Porter	Capt.Bradley	Wireless Tactical Observation.	5.am	7.25am	Successful
,, 1869	Lt.Grattan-Bellew	-:-	-:-	8.45am / 7.30am	11.30am / 9.30am	-:-
,, 1857	Lt.MacDonald	Capt.Howell.	-:-	6.20am / 1.50pm	8.am / 4.25pm	-:-
,, 1869	Lt.Grattan-Bellew	Lt.Gordon.	-:-	4.pm	6.25pm	-:-
BE2c. 1676	Capt.Playfair	Lt.Coventry	Attempted Reconnaissance	5.35pm	7.pm	Unsuccessful. Engine failed at BAILLEUL. 1 copy of report to 1st Army, 2 copies to 1st Advanced Wing
Voisin 1879	Lt.Braithwaite	2/Lt.Holmes	Reconnaissance	4.50pm	7.5pm	

Major.R.F.C.
O.C.No.16.Squadron.R.F.C.

Figure 15   16 Squadron summary of work showing Alan Geoffrey Fox as missing (AIR 1/1253/204/8/9)

8.4 Royal Air Force

The creation of the RAF in April 1918 saw a number of changes made to the titles of units which had formerly been part of the RNAS. Since the changes made upon creation of the RAF, further evolutionary changes have occurred during the history of the RAF and these will be noted in the relevant sections.

8.4.1 First World War

The RAF operational records are in AIR 1 together with those of the RFC and RNAS. The most important item to note when looking for squadron records after April 1918 is that former RNAS squadrons were renumbered into the 200 numerical range. Therefore, 1 Squadron RNAS became 210 Squadron RAF.

Accounts of the experiences of a number of RFC/RAF officers who attended the RAF Staff College after the First World War can be found in AIR 1.

Locations of RFC/RAF between February 1917 and September 1918 are listed in AIR 1/2112/207/52.

8.4.2 Inter war years

The Royal Air Force carried out a wide variety of operations, both peaceable and offensive, between the end of the First World War and the beginning of the Second World War.

An example of the non-belligerent operations was the RAF involvement in pioneering work with regard to the planning and trial of air routes for civil airliners. The RAF undertook experiments with aircraft design and achieved various record successes with regard to altitude, long distance and other experimental flying. Many records concerning this aspect of the RAF's activities during this period can be found in AIR 2, AIR 5, AIR 8, and the Operational Record Books in AIR 27 and AIR 29.

Offensive operations undertaken by the RAF, by both armoured cars and aircraft, occurred over much of the Empire as well as in countries which had been involved in the First World War. The Operational Record Books of Armoured Car Units can be found in AIR 29.

Operations in both North and South Russia continued until 1919 and numerous operations in Mesopotamia (later Iraq), Kurdistan, Persia (later Iran) and India went on sporadically until 1940.

In early 1920 the RAF was involved in operations in Somaliland, which finally led to the defeat of the 'Mad Mullah', who had been causing the British many problems since 1900.

Documents recording and describing the operations during this time are distributed amongst a number of different record classes. AIR 1 contains numerous files relating to North and South Russia, Kurdistan and Mesopotamia. AIR 2 covers the same areas as AIR 1 and also holds files concerning Somaliland. AIR 5 contains files on Somaliland, Iraq and India.

8.4.2.1 North and South Russia

Reports on operations in South Russia can be found in AIR 1/408/15/232/6–8. The war diary for South Russia is in AIR 1/2375/226/11/1–5. Nominal rolls of other ranks and officers in the region are in AIR 1/1666/204/99/12 and 13 respectively.

Operational records from North Russia are in AIR 1/435/15/274/2–3 and AIR 1/438. Syren Force records can be found in AIR 1/472/15/312/167 and 168 and AIR 1/473/15/312/174.

Despatches covering operations in North and South Russia are in AIR 5/1340.

8.4.2.2 Somaliland

Operations by twelve DH 9as of the specially formed Z Unit RAF, against the 'Mad Mullah', were very important as they were the first independent operations undertaken by the RAF, in what was to be its prime role between 1918 and 1939, that of colonial policing.

References to this operation can be found in AIR 5/846, 1309–1315 and 1422. (See Figure 16 for the unit war diary in AIR 5/1309.) The files include operations orders, medical reports and photographs, observers' reports, a war dairy (which interestingly lists all the jobs undertaken by the RAF airmen) and despatches.

The medal roll for the Africa General Service Medal with Somaliland 1920 clasp is in AIR 2/2270. The recommendations for honours and awards granted for services during the operation can be found in AIR 2/204.

8.4.2.3 Mesopotamia

A summary of the campaign can be found in AIR 1/674/21/6/87. War diaries are in AIR 1/21/15/1/109, AIR 1/426/15/206/1 and AIR 1/432/15/260/23–25. A report by the Mesopotamia Commission on operations in the region is in AIR 1/2357/226/5/18.

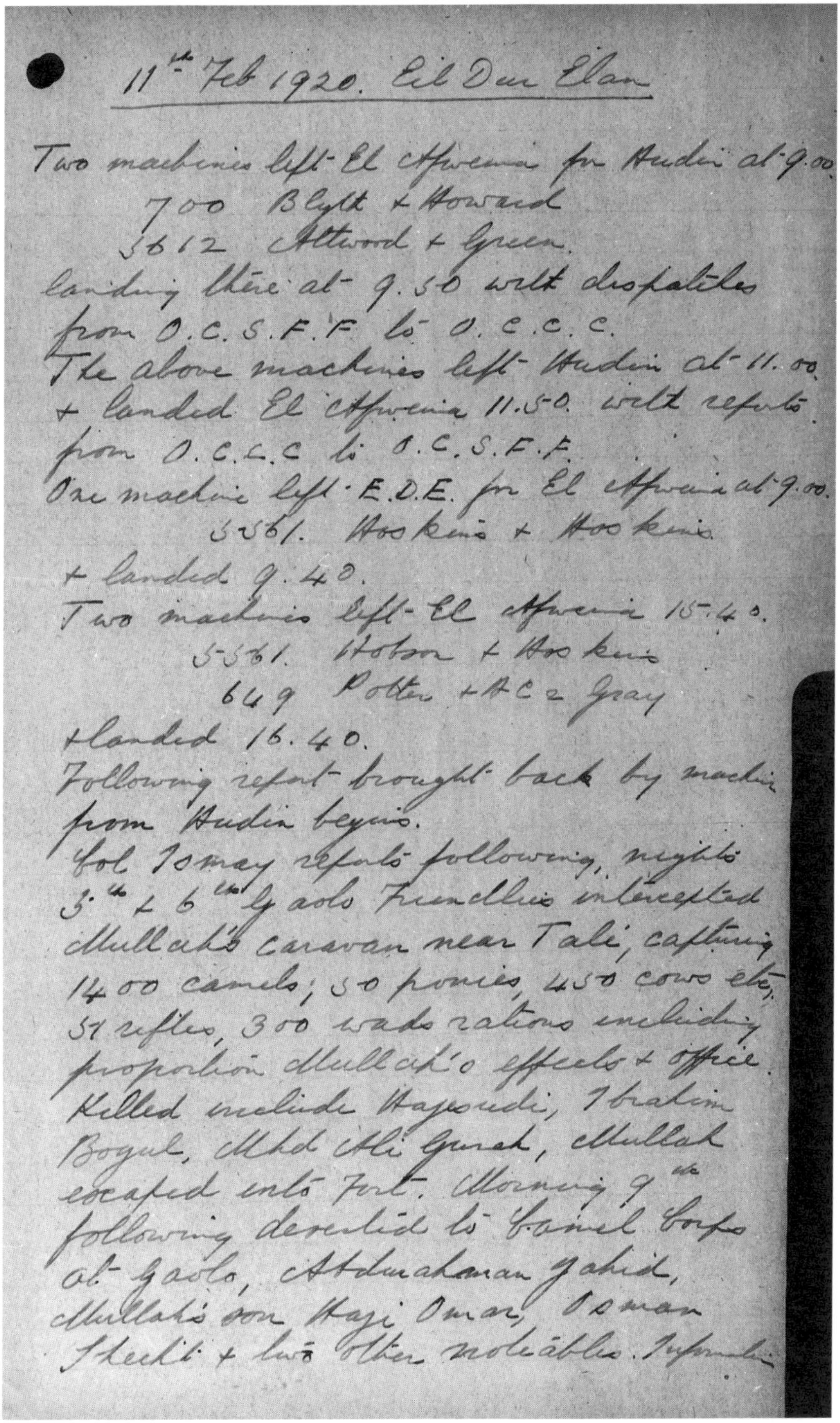

11th Feb 1920. Eil Dur Elan

Two machines left El Afweina for Hudin at 9.00.
700 Blyth + Howard
3612 Attwood + Green.
landing there at 9.50 with despatches
from O.C.S.F.F. to O.C.C.C.
The above machines left Hudin at 11.00
+ landed El Afweina 11.50. with reports
from O.C.C.C. to O.C.S.F.F.
One machine left E.D.E. for El Afweina at 9.00.
3561. Hoskins + Hoskins
+ landed 9.40.
Two machines left El Afweina 15.40.
5561. Hobson + Hoskins
649 Potter + AC2 Gray
+ landed 16.40.
Following report brought back by machine
from Hudin begins.
For 10 may reports following. nights
5th + 6th gaols Friendlies intercepted
Mullah's caravan near Tali, capturing
1400 camels; 50 ponies, 450 cows etc.,
51 rifles, 300 wads rations including
proportion Mullah's effects + office.
Killed include Hajsudi, Ibrahim
Bogul, Mhd Ali Gunah, Mullah
escaped into fort. Morning 9th
following deserted to friendli troops
at gaolo, Abdurahman Yahid,
Mullah's son Haji Omar, Osman
Shehli + two other notiables. September

Figure 16 Unit war diary for operations in Somaliland, 1920 (AIR 5/1309)

Files of the RAF control of Mesopotamia are in AIR 5/224 and 476.

8.4.2.4 Kurdistan

Squadrons involved in operations in this region included 6, 30 and 63 Squadrons. Despatches concerning operations in this region in 1923 and 1924 can be found in AIR 1/2132/207/136/2 and AIR 5/292.

8.4.2.5 Iraq

Squadrons involved in various operations in Iraq included 6, 30, 55, 63, 70 and 84 Squadrons. Of all the operations in Iraq, the most significant occurred between 1928 and 1935. Most of the operational records concerning Iraq are in AIR 5. Of these the most significant are AIR 5/344, 460 and 544, AIR 5/1253-1255 and AIR 5/1287-1294. Squadron operational records can be found in AIR 27

Photographs of southern Iraq between 1919 and 1929 can be found in AIR 5/842.

Unit records of a number of Armoured Car Companies which served in Iraq can be found in AIR 29/50–53.

8.4.2.6 India

Numerous operations against various tribes in India and Afghanistan were undertaken between 1919 and 1940. The majority occured in the North Western Frontier of India.

Organizational records of the RAF in India between 1918 and 1919 can be found in AIR 2/68, with a resumé of RFC operations in AIR 2/123.

A despatch from the Commander in Chief India, concerning the Third Afghan War in 1919, is in AIR 1/2132/207/136/1. Notes from war diaries of Waziritsan Force I 1919 and 1920 are in AIR 1/423/15/251/1.

Air operations which took place between 1922 and 1928 are covered in AIR 5/298.

A fuller history of all RAF operations in India can be found in AIR 5/1321–1337.

Reports on India between 1921 and 1930, including a report from Air Vice Marshall Salmond, are in AIR 8/46. A memorandum on the use of air power in India is in AIR 8/83.

Records of operations on the North West Frontier of India between 1937 and 1939 are in AIR 8/529.

8.4.2.7 Palestine

Pre-war operations in Palestine covered the period 19 April 1936 to 3 September 1939. Numerous RAF units saw service in the region during this time. Of these the following squadrons are known to have served there: 6, 14, 33, 80, 208, 211 and 216 Squadrons RAF.

A despatch concerning RAF operations in Palestine in 1936 is in AIR 2/1938. Monthly summaries of RAF activities between 1930 and 1939 are in AIR 5/1245–1248, with further operational reports in AIR 5/1244.

8.4.3 Second World War

Operational records of the RAF between 1939 and 1945 can be found in a number of different sources. The records listed below are primarily those operational records where information concerning individuals may be found. Those in this section are more useful in gaining a general knowledge of operations.

As part of King's Regulations of the RAF it was a requirement that all commands, groups, stations, wings, squadrons and all miscellaneous units had to complete RAF Forms 540 and 541. Forms 540 were for monthly summaries and were completed by all units. Forms 541 were daily summaries and were completed by units such as RAF squadrons.

Records which cover more than just specific units or organizations include Combat Reports in AIR 50, which are arranged by unit and include a number of Fleet Air Arm squadrons and other non-RAF units.

Intelligence records concerning RAF operations, especially those with special force, can be found in AIR 40 and AIR 20.

There are numerous records, relating to a variety of specific as well as general operations, distributed amongst the AIR record classes. At the end of the war a number of narratives relating to air operations were compiled and these can be found in AIR 41.

The records of the 2nd Tactical Air Force, which was responsible for operations from airfields in North Western Europe after D-Day, are in AIR 37.

8.4.3.1 Commands

As commands were the highest link in the administrative chain of command in the sole hands of the RAF, they kept separate records rather than just Operational Record Books (ORBs). The table below shows where these are command papers are now located.

Command	Reference
Balloon Command	AIR 13
Bomber Command	AIR 14
Coastal Command	AIR 15
Fighter Command	AIR 16
Maintenance Command	AIR 17
Overseas Commands	AIR 23
Air Training Command	AIR 32
Ferry and Transport Command	AIR 38
Army Co-operation Command	AIR 39

Of all of these commands, the records of those actually involved in operations are the most expansive and extensive. When completing research into a particular incident it may be necessary to consult the Command papers for certain details.

The ORBs of commands can be found in AIR 24 and are arranged alphabetically by name of command and then chronologically under each command. Included in AIR 24 are the record books of the Director of the Women's Auxiliary Air Force.

8.4.3.2 Groups

The ORBs of RAF groups are in AIR 25. These records are arranged numerically by number of the group, and the type of group, be it a fighter or bomber group, for example, is mentioned in the class list.

8.4.3.3 Wings

The ORBs for wings can be found in AIR 26. These records are arranged in numerical order by the number of the wing. However the class list does note the type of wing, whether it be a fighter, signal or overseas wing, for example. Apart from a few instances individuals are rarely mentioned.

In many instances wings fed information relating to operations up the chain of command through group and up to command. It is therefore possible to find the activities of wings in group and command records.

8.4.3.4 Squadrons

Squadron ORBs are by far the most informative of all RAF unit records. These books record the sorties of each unit, giving the aircraft type, unit callsign or aircraft serial number, crew (by name), task or target, weapon load, time of take off and time of return. If the aircraft did not return, this is also recorded. The arrival and departure of personnel joining and leaving the unit is usually recorded, as are details concerning awards.

The records in AIR 27 can be used to create a list of all the flying operations that RAF aircrew completed.

Operational records concerning units who flew on behalf of SOE (Special Operations Executive) can be found in AIR 20.

A typical example of an RAF squadron ORB can be seen in Figure 17.

8.4.3.5 Stations

The station ORBs are in AIR 28 and are arranged in alphabetical order. The AIR 28 class list contains an alphabetical index. Station 540s record numerous incidents which affected them, and in many cases it is in the station ORB that details concerning Courts of Inquiry may be found. Individuals are frequently mentioned in station ORBs.

Photographs of RAF air stations can be found in AIR 20/7585 (A–I) and AIR 207586 (K–Z).

8.4.3.6 Other units

The ORBs of all those RAF units which may be called miscellaneous but are no less important can be found in AIR 29. Amongst the units to be found in AIR 29 are RAF regiments, air sea rescue flights, operational training and conversion units and other flying training units.

8.4.4 Since 1945

Researching records for post-1945 operations can be done by consulting the class lists for all of those records which covered the Second World War or by using the 'On-line Lists'. Numerous records exist for operations in Malaya, Korea, Borneo, the Middle East and Kenya. The squadron records in AIR 27 and other units in AIR 29 all contain records of this period.

Bn. P.—3384 (G 1)—1.4.43—50,000 copies.

OPERATIONS RECORD BOOK.

AIR FORCE (INDIA) FORM 541.

Appendix.................

DETAIL OF WORK CARRIED OUT.

By NO. 159 SQUADRON.....R.A.F

From......hrs....../......to......hrs....../..../......   No. of pages used for day............

Aircraft Type and No.	Crew.	Duty.	Time Up.	Time Down.	Remarks.	References.
Liberator BZ.924."F".	F/O.G.Pendleton (Capt) F/O.Quinn (Co-p.) F/O.T.Titchmarsh(Nav.) F/S.R.H.Pryde. (1stWop) Sgt.A.H.Allanach(2ndWop) Sgt.J.Tutty. (M.U.) F/S.R.Wood. (B.G.) Sgt.P.J.Clay. (R.G.) Sgt.P.J.Bailey(F/E)		17.02	02.21	NIGHT OF 21st/22nd FEBRUARY, 1944. Load: As for aircraft "X". 1st run, 20.47 hrs. 10000 ft. 160 IAS. 320 Mag. 2nd run, 20.54 hrs. 10000 ft. 160 IAS. 355 Mag. ATTACKING SAGAING SHORE RAILWAY STATION. First and second sticks aimed at Shore Railway Station. First and second runs, bursts seen believed across target.	Appendix F. Page 10
Liberator BZ.962 "D".	P/O.A.Black (Capt.) F/S.R.H.Simmons (Co-p) P/O.J.G.Portch (Nav.) W/O.C.A.Morgan (1stWop) F/S.C.R.Church (2ndWop) F/Sgt.W.Lear (M.U.) Sgt.F.Holroyd (B.G.) F/S.P.J.O'Keefe(R.G.) Sgt.Bavistock		17.00	02.12	Load: As for aircraft "W". 1st run, 20.45 hrs. 0500 ft. 160 IAS. 350 Mag. 2nd run, 21.10 hrs. 0000 ft. 155 IAS. 003 Mag. ATTACKING SAGAING SHORE RAILWAY STATION. First and second sticks aimed at Shore Railway Station. First run, bursts seen – first on target remainder overshot. Second run, bursts seen parallel with bank in target area.	"
Libertor BZ. 980."A".	W/O.J.C.Stuart (Capt.) P/O.Heynert (Co-p) W/O.A.Longworth (Nav.) F/S.W.Etherington(1stWop) Sgt.R.M.Hill (2ndWop) F/O.R.T.Hocking(M.U.) Sgt.A.H.Maude (B.G.) F/Sgt.C.Kirby		16.52	01.45	Load: As for aircraft "X". 1st run, 20.39 hrs. 1.200 ft. 160 IAS. 330 Mag. 2nd run, 20.42 hrs. 1.200 ft. 160 IAS. 175 Mag. ATTACKING SAGAING SHORE RAILWAY STATION. First and second sticks aimed at Shore Railway Station. First run, 2 bursts seen immediately N. of point of aim. Second run, all bursts seen in target area.	"

Figure 17 A typical example of an RAF Squadron Operational Record Book (AIR 27/10▪1)

8.5 Fleet Air Arm

The formal return to Admiralty control of the Fleet Air Arm (FAA) just prior to the Second World War means that operational records of the service may be found in the ADM and AIR record classes, as described in the following sections.

8.5.1 Second World War

Operational records of the FAA are primarily to be found in four Admiralty record classes (ADM 1, ADM 116, ADM 199 and ADM 207) and two Air Ministry record classes (AIR 27, AIR 50).

ORBs of some FAA squadrons can be found in ADM 207. However, the class does not have all of the FAA ORBs. These records usually note the sorties, crew, and hours flown on sorties, and many contain additional notes relating to operations. A number of FAA ORBs can be found in AIR 27/2386 and 2387.

Reports of proceedings of FAA squadrons can be found in ADM 199. Rather than being completed on a day-to-day basis as ORBs were, the reports of proceedings were compiled from a number of different sources and accompanied by an overview by the commanding officer. The reports of proceedings only covered a short duration, consequently it may be necessary to obtain a number of these reports to create a complete operational history of a unit. A report of proceedings concerning the attack on Taranto can be found in ADM 199/167.

In many cases the activities of FAA squadrons can also be found by locating the records of the ships from which they operated. Many of these reports can be found in ADM 199. A report concerning the sinking of the *Bismarck* and the involvement of 818 and 820 squadrons can found by looking at the report written by the CO of HMS *Ark Royal* in ADM 199/657.

Ships' logs which contain very brief details about operational activities can be found in ADM 53.

Reports concerning specific operations or events such as the attack on Taranto or the sinking of the *Bismarck*, for example, may be found in ADM 1, Series 1, Codes 3 and 90 and ADM 116, Codes 3 and 90. Reports concerning the attack on Taranto can be found in ADM 1/11182, ADM 223/336 and ADM 234/325.

Many operations during the Second World War were given codenames which can be used to identify relevant records. The FAA attack on Taranto was codenamed

'Judgement' and the FAA attack on the *Tirpitz* in April 1944 was codenamed 'Tungsten'. Records concerning Operation Tungsten can be found in ADM 1/15695, ADM 1/15806, ADM 199/941 and ADM 237/345.

An example of an FAA squadron's report of proceedings (ADM 199/167) can be seen in Figure 18.

8.5.2 Since 1945

FAA operational records after 1945 can be found in the record classes used for Second World War records but they are primarily to be found in ADM 1 and ADM 116. A new post-war record class, ADM 335 Fleet Air Arm Operational Records, also contains material of the post-war era up to the 1960s.

8.6 Glider Pilot Regiment and Army Air Corps

As the dual role of the Glider Pilot Regiment (GPR) and Army Air Corps (AAC) covered both the air and ground, consequently records relating to their operational activities may be found in both AIR and WO record classes. In some cases the activities of these units were controlled by Headquarters Combined Operations, whose records can be found in DEFE 2.

8.6.1 Second World War

As units of the GPR and AAC had specific titles and they took part in military operations which were given codenames, it is these which can be used to identify and obtain records concerning their activities.

Operational Record Books of AAC Air Observation Post (AOP) squadrons can be found in AIR 27. AOP squadrons were numbered between 651 and 660. Further details about the numbering of AOP squadrons can be found in *RAF Squadrons* by Jefford.

Operational Record Books of glider units, including squadrons and training units, can be found in AIR 29.

Unit War Diaries of army units in the Second World War are arranged by operational theatre and then by unit. A number of diaries concerning glider units can be found in WO 166 (Home Forces), WO 169 (North Africa), WO 170 (Italy) and WO 171 (North Western Europe).

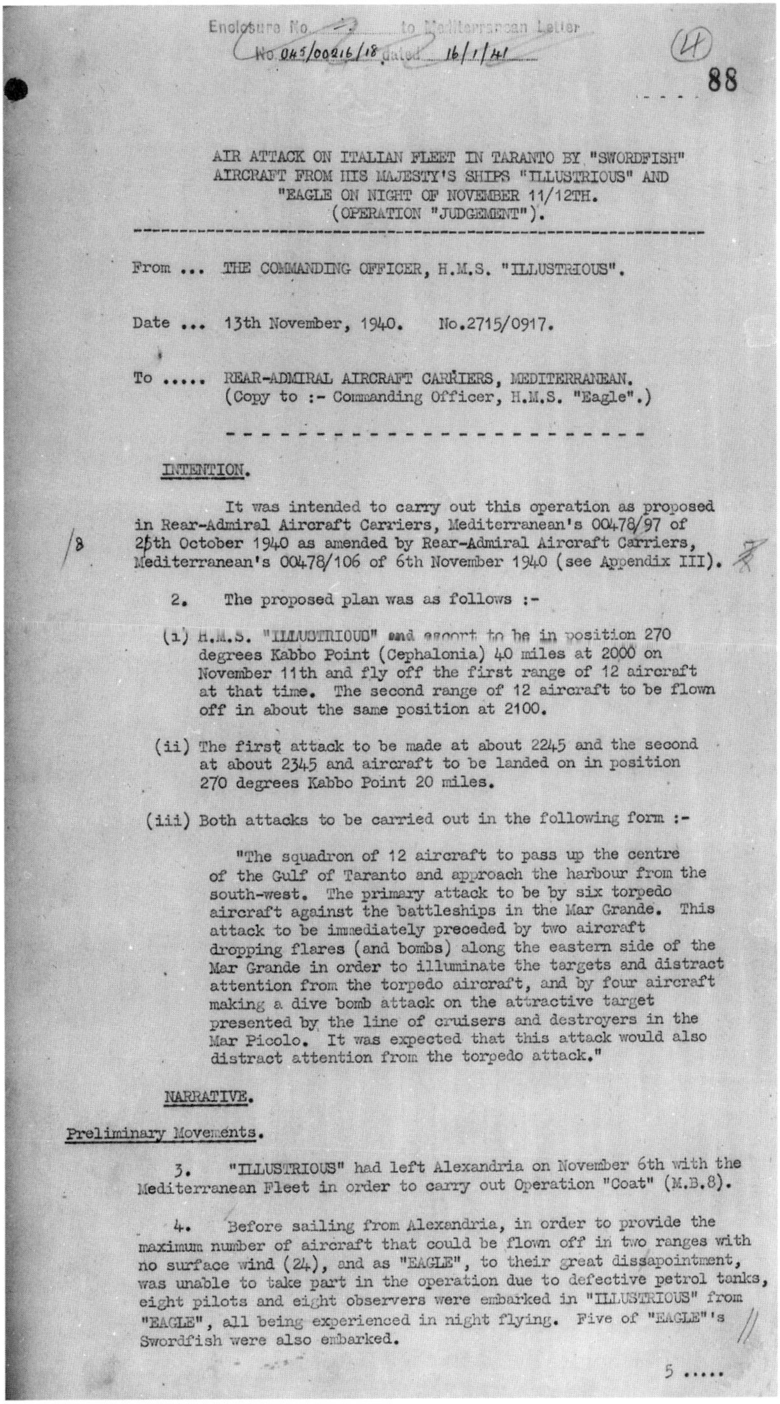

Enclosure No. ___ to Mediterranean Letter
No. 04*/00216/18 dated 16/1/41

④

88

AIR ATTACK ON ITALIAN FLEET IN TARANTO BY "SWORDFISH"
AIRCRAFT FROM HIS MAJESTY'S SHIPS "ILLUSTRIOUS" AND
"EAGLE ON NIGHT OF NOVEMBER 11/12TH.
(OPERATION "JUDGEMENT").

From ... THE COMMANDING OFFICER, H.M.S. "ILLUSTRIOUS".

Date ... 13th November, 1940.   No.2715/0917.

To ..... REAR-ADMIRAL AIRCRAFT CARRIERS, MEDITERRANEAN.
(Copy to :- Commanding Officer, H.M.S. "Eagle".)

- -

<u>INTENTION.</u>

It was intended to carry out this operation as proposed
in Rear-Admiral Aircraft Carriers, Mediterranean's 00478/97 of
25th October 1940 as amended by Rear-Admiral Aircraft Carriers,
Mediterranean's 00478/106 of 6th November 1940 (see Appendix III).

2.   The proposed plan was as follows :-

(i) H.M.S. "ILLUSTRIOUS" and escort to be in position 270
degrees Kabbo Point (Cephalonia) 40 miles at 2000 on
November 11th and fly off the first range of 12 aircraft
at that time. The second range of 12 aircraft to be flown
off in about the same position at 2100.

(ii) The first attack to be made at about 2245 and the second
at about 2345 and aircraft to be landed on in position
270 degrees Kabbo Point 20 miles.

(iii) Both attacks to be carried out in the following form :-

"The squadron of 12 aircraft to pass up the centre
of the Gulf of Taranto and approach the harbour from the
south-west. The primary attack to be by six torpedo
aircraft against the battleships in the Mar Grande. This
attack to be immediately preceded by two aircraft
dropping flares (and bombs) along the eastern side of the
Mar Grande in order to illuminate the targets and distract
attention from the torpedo aircraft, and by four aircraft
making a dive bomb attack on the attractive target
presented by the line of cruisers and destroyers in the
Mar Picolo. It was expected that this attack would also
distract attention from the torpedo attack."

<u>NARRATIVE.</u>

<u>Preliminary Movements.</u>

3.   "ILLUSTRIOUS" had left Alexandria on November 6th with the
Mediterranean Fleet in order to carry out Operation "Coat" (M.B.8).

4.   Before sailing from Alexandria, in order to provide the
maximum number of aircraft that could be flown off in two ranges with
no surface wind (24), and as "EAGLE", to their great dissapointment,
was unable to take part in the operation due to defective petrol tanks,
eight pilots and eight observers were embarked in "ILLUSTRIOUS" from
"EAGLE", all being experienced in night flying. Five of "EAGLE"'s
Swordfish were also embarked.

5 .....

Figure 18 FAA Squadron report of proceedings, in this case for the
attack on Taranto, November 1940 (ADM 199/167)

Operations which involved the GPR include Operation Freshman, the attempted attack on a heavy water plant at Vermortt in Norway, Operation Husky, the invasion of Sicily, Operation Overlord, the Normandy invasion, Operation Market Garden, the airborne landing at Arnhem and Operation Varsity, the crossing of the Rhine. There are numerous files concerning the GPR/AAC part in these operations but some of the most significant are listed below.

8.6.1.1 Freshman

The main records can be found in AIR 20/3648, 4527 and 11930, AIR 39/45 and 147, DEFE 2/219–224 and 1408 and HS 2/184. For the records concerning the war crimes committed in connection with this operation see Section 12.3.

8.6.1.2. Husky

The main records can be found in AIR 8/1015 and 1316, AIR 20/2585 and 4475–4477, AIR 23/5527, WO 106/3877, WO 201/659 and WO 204/1072.

8.6.1.3 Overlord

There are thousands of files concerning the Normandy invasion. Those applicable to the GPR include WO 205/78–80, WO 219/222–226 and WO 219/2180.

8.6.1.4 Market Garden

The main records can be found in AIR 37/1214 and 1249, AIR 67/32 and WO 205/870.

8.6.1.5 Varsity

The main records can be found in AIR 14/1438, AIR 20/4314, AIR 37/56, 57, 267, 268, 304, 305, 326, 327, 543, 907, 909 and 1128, WO 106/5847, WO 205/200–204, 951 and 952.

The Aircrew Log Book of Staff Sergeant D.W. Lee, 1 Battalion Glider Pilot Regiment, can be found in AIR 4/59.

8.6.2 Since 1945

Post-war activities of the AAC can once again be found in AIR 27 and WO 233. The papers of the Sixth Airborne Division in Palestine between 1945 and 1948, which included men of the AAC, may be found in WO 275.

9 Casualties and air crashes

9.1 Casualties

Loss of life, through flying accidents or through enemy action, is unfortunately a common occurrence in the history of aviation. The following records, whilst recording the demise of thousands of individuals, do at least enable researchers to create a more complete picture of the career of a member of the flying services.

9.1.1 First World War

Information concerning commissioned and warrant officers and ratings who died from whatever cause, be it illness or through enemy action, can be found in ADM 242. There is an officers' card index in the Research Enquiries Room, ADM 242/1–6. This is arranged alphabetically and shows name, date, place and cause of death. The War Graves roll in ADM 242/7–10, covering all ranks, gives rank or rating, date of birth, date and place of death and the name and address of next of kin.

Numerous files concerning casualties can be found in AIR 1 by using the keyword 'casualties' on the 'On-line Lists'. Amongst the files to be found are many concerning officers who are missing, presumed dead.

Dead of the RFC and RAF can be found by using *Soldiers Died in the Great War*, which is available on CD ROM in the Library. The second source to consult is *Airmen Died in the Great War* by Chris Hobson, a copy of which is available in the Library. To find out where an individual is buried or commemorated try using the Commonwealth War Graves Commission website (www.cwgc.org) and search their on-line registers.

The RAF Museum holds a number of casualty cards concerning RFC and RAF casualties of the First World War. In many cases a card will provide the unit, date and place of death and other basic biographical data. See Section 15.6 for details on the RAF Museum.

Statistics of casualties incurred by the RFC/RAF during the First World War can be found in AIR 1/39/15/7. A list of Americans who died whilst serving with the RFC/RAF can be found in AIR 2/219. A list of casualties, both military and civil, incurred during air raids and shore bombardments between December 1914 and June 1918, can be found in AIR 1/604/16/15/235.

French or Belgian death certificates of men who died in France or Belgium but outside of the area of operations can be found in RG 35/45–49.

9.1.2 Inter war years

Specific casualty records for the inter war years (1919–38) are not easily located. If a death occurred in a given unit, you can consult the unit records to see if anything is mentioned. The casualty records of the Royal Navy, and therefore the Fleet Air Arm, continue after the First World War in ADM 104. The Commonwealth War Graves Commission does hold some data relating to deaths between 1919 and 1938.

9.1.3 Second World War

During the Second World War over 55 000 aircrew lost their lives, as a result of enemy action, in accidents or through other circumstances. An initial consultation of the Commonwealth War Graves Commission records, either by letter or by using their website (see Section 15.7), will provide the researcher with much useful data. Beyond name, rank, date of death and place of commemoration or burial, the CWGC records may also provide the researcher with the all important unit details. Once a unit is identified, then the relevant unit and operational records can be consulted (see Chapter 8).

Unit operational records may provide not only personal details but also the cause of death, be it in action or otherwise. As there were so many flying accidents during the Second World War, very few of the accident inquiry records have survived. Depending upon the location of the accident, it may be possible to find brief details in the RAF Station Operational Record Books in AIR 28.

Doing a keyword search on the 'On-line Lists' using the term 'Casualty' or 'Casualties' will produce plenty of results. An example of a record that could be found as a result of such a search is AIR 16/609 which contains the 'Aircrew casualty statistics for Battle of Britain'.

The Roll of Honour for army deaths in the Second World War is in WO 304. This roll is arranged in alphabetical order and the information contained in it is numerically coded. An explanatory guide to these codes is available in the Research Enquiries Room.

Casualty records of the Royal Navy and consequently the Fleet Air Arm are in ADM 104. Once again these records are arranged alphabetically.

The RAF Museum at Hendon holds a number of casualty cards relating to 1939–1945. For more information about accessing the RAF Museum archive see Section 15.6.

9.1.4 Since 1945

Very few specific casualty records for the post-1945 period are yet available. By far the most useful sources are the operational records. See Chapter 8 for further details.

9.2 Air crashes

Although there are policy files concerning air crashes in a number of different AIR and AVIA record classes, the records in AVIA 5, Ministry of Aviation Accident Investigation Branch, contain detailed reports about crashes involving military aircraft from 1919 to the post-Second World War period. The records in AVIA 5 provide aircraft serial number and type, names of crew and a detailed analysis of the cause of the crash with appropriate recommendations. If you know the serial number of the aircraft involved in a particular crash you can use it as a keyword to search the 'On-line Lists'.

The Admiralty also carried out investigations into their crashed aircraft. However, unlike the records in AVIA 5, the records in ADM 1 only really cover the post-1945 period. This is because prior to the Second World War the aircraft of the Royal Navy were administered by the RAF. As with AVIA 5 you can use an aircraft serial number as a keyword when searching the 'On-line Lists'.

10 Medals and awards

10.1 Introduction

Medals can be split into a number of different groups depending upon the purpose for which they were awarded. In this chapter it is intended to describe the three most important groups and the records associated with them.

10.2 Campaign medals

Campaign medals are those medals which are awarded to an individual for being present in a theatre of operations and in some cases taking part in particular battles. In some cases a medal only was issued denoting which campaign an individual was involved in. In lengthier campaigns it was also possible to receive clasps to a medal, denoting particular places or dates where and when an individual was involved. There are a variety of different campaign medals which have been issued for numerous campaigns since 1793. As British military aviation is a comparatively new part of warfare, so the campaigns in which aviation first took part were only quite recent.

Such was the complicated nature of the origins of the manpower of the RE Balloon Section, but more importantly the Royal Flying Corps, Royal Naval Air Service and the Royal Air Force, that many members of these organizations saw active service with other units prior to getting involved in aviation. Many men received campaign and other medals with their previous units. These awards are not discussed here. For more information about medals awarded to members of the British Army see *Army Records for Family Historians* by Simon Fowler and the present author and for those with a Royal Navy or Royal Marine background, see *Naval Records for Genealogists* by N.A.M. Rodger

10.2.1 Royal Engineers Balloon Section

Prior to the formation of the RFC in 1912, all campaign service was undertaken by the Royal Engineers Balloon Section. Although this section was involved in a number of different military operations around the world prior to 1912, its men were only awarded campaign medals for three different campaigns.

The first campaign medal men of the RE Balloon Section were awarded was the Egypt Medal 1882–9, for services in eastern Sudan in 1885. The roll for this medal can be found in WO 100/64 ff80. The medal roll lists the name, rank and number of all those men of the section who were entitled to the medal.

After service in the eastern Sudan the next campaign in which balloons were involved was the South African or Boer War 1899–1902. Three sections of balloons took part in the war, all of those men who served in South Africa being awarded the Queen's South Africa Medal. The medal rolls for this medal can be found in WO 100/160. Not only does the medal roll list the names of those who were eligible for the medal, it also notes the particular clasps an individual was entitled to, thereby signifying where in South Africa he served.

The third and final campaign which resulted in men of the RE Balloon Section being awarded a campaign medal was the Boxer Rebellion or Third China War in 1900. As the majority of their resources were in use in South Africa, the number of RE Balloon Section men who saw service in China was very few. The medal roll for the Third China Medal can be found in WO 100/95.

10.2.2 Royal Flying Corps

Medal rolls relating to campaign medals won by members of the Royal Flying Corps are restricted to two record classes: WO 100 for non-First World War medal records; and WO 329 for First World War campaign medal rolls.

10.2.2.1 First World War medals and Silver War Badge

Six different campaign medals were awarded for service during the First World War and, apart from in exceptional cases, the maximum number of medals which could be awarded to an individual was three. The medals were: the 1914 Star, the 1914/15 Star, the British War Medal 1914–20, the Victory Medal 1914–19, the Territorial Force War Medal 1914–19 and the Mercantile Marine War Medal. The last named medal was awarded exclusively to members of the Merchant Navy, and although really outside of the scope of this book, it may be possible to find men of the RFC, RNAS and RAF who qualified for the medal prior to joining the armed forces.

The 1914 Star, authorized in 1917, was awarded for service in France and Belgium between 5 August and 22 November 1914. In 1919 a bar with the inscription '5th Aug. – 22nd Nov. 1914' was sanctioned. Only those personnel who had actually been under fire during the above specified dates were eligible. The 1914 Star was not awarded on its own; it should always be accompanied by the British War and Victory Medals.

The 1914/15 Star, authorized in 1918, was awarded for service in France and Belgium after 22 November 1914 until 31 December 1915, and in all other operational theatres around the world from 5 August 1914 until 31 December 1915. The 1914/15 Star was not awarded to those personnel who had already qualified for the 1914 Star. As with the 1914 Star, the 1914/15 Star should always be accompanied by the British War and Victory Medals.

The British War Medal 1914–20 (BWM) was sanctioned in 1919. Qualification for the medal varied slightly depending upon which service the individual was in. Men of the army, including the RFC, had to have entered a theatre of war or rendered approved service overseas between 5 August 1914 and 11 November 1918. Service in Russia in 1919 and 1920 also qualified for the award.

The Victory Medal (VM), also authorized in 1919, was awarded to those personnel who served on the establishment of a unit in an operational theatre. This medal could not be awarded alone but must always be accompanied by the British War Medal.

The Territorial Force War Medal 1914–19 (TFWM) was awarded to members or former members of the Territorial Force only. To qualify for the award an individual had to have been a member of the Territorial Force on or prior to 30 September 1914, and to have served in an operational theatre outside of the United Kingdom between 5 August 1914 and 11 November 1918. Those men who qualified for either the 1914 or 1914/15 Star could not receive this medal.

The Mercantile Marine War Medal 1914–18 was issued by the Board of Trade to personnel of the Merchant Navy who sailed on at least one voyage through a danger area.

The Silver War Badge (SWB), authorized in September 1916, was given to all military personnel who were discharged because of sickness or wounds contracted or received as a result of war service, either at home or overseas at any time after 4 August 1914. The majority of Silver War Badge rolls in WO 329 are for men discharged from the RFC.

The following table gives the PRO references for those medal rolls that specifically concern the RFC and RAF:

Reference	Medal roll
WO 329/2504	1914 Star RFC other ranks
WO 329/2512	1914 Star RFC officers
WO 329/2926–2930	1914/15 Star RFC other ranks
WO 329/2135	BWM and VM RFC other ranks
WO 329/2136–2137	BWM and VM RAF other ranks

WO 329/3270   TFWM RAF
WO 329/3244   SWB RFC

10.2.2.2 How to use the First World War medal rolls (WO 329)

To search the medal rolls in WO 329, it is necessary to consult the Medal Index Cards (MIC) in the class WO 372 first. These cards are on microfiche and are held in the Microfilm Reading Room.

WO 372 is an alphabetical list of those individuals who qualified for any of the following campaign medals: 1914 Star, 1914/15 Star, British War Medal 1914–20, Victory Medal 1914–19, Territorial Force War Medal 1914–19 and/or were awarded a Silver War Badge.

The MICs are in alphabetical sequence and Regimental Order of Precedence. Names of individuals are usually listed in the following format:

> Jones J
> Jones James
> Jones John
> Jones Julius
> Jones James A
> Jones John A
> Jones Julius A
> Jones James B
> Jones John B
> Jones Julius B
> Jones James A B
> Jones John A B

This sequence of surname, followed by single initial, followed by single forename, followed by forename and initial(s), is used throughout the MICs. Each sequence of names is also listed in Regimental Order of Precedence, whereby those men who served in the most senior regiment in the army appear first and men from the second most senior and subsequent regiments appear in a specific order (see Section 10.2.2.4).

On each MIC the following information is given: surname, first forename, name or initial and subsequent initials, rank, regiment, service number, the medals to which the individual was entitled and the Army Medal Office medal roll references for these medals, the name or number of the first operational theatre in which the individual first served, and the date when the individual first entered that theatre. Usually the name of the theatre is given in full but in some cases just a number and/or letter is given. There were 26 different operational theatres, details of which can be found in

Section 10.2.2.3. The Army Medal Office references usually appear in the form of an alpha-numeric code, the last part of which is the page number on which the name of the individual appears.

The MICs were filmed onto sheets of microfiche and each sheet contains 360 MICs. When the MICs were filmed they were laid out in a specific pattern.

In order to obtain the correct WO 329 references for the medal rolls and Silver War Badge roll, the sequence to use is as follows:

- Find the sheet of microfiche which includes the surname of the individual you are interested in.
- Find the name of the individual on the MIC.
- Write down the details of Army Medal Office reference numbers, which are noted alongside the names of the medals an individual was awarded.
- Change the Army Medal Office references into WO 329 references using the WO 329/1 key, which is available in the Microfilm Reading Room, as a copied bound volume.
- Order the WO 329 volume you require on one of the computer terminals in the Research Enquiries Room.

It is possible to obtain photocopies of both the MICs and the medal rolls. Please speak to the staff in the Microfilm Reading Room .

10.2.2.3 Operational theatres of war 1914–20

The alpha-numeric codes for each theatre of war, e.g. 1a relating to service in France and Belgium in the Western European theatre of war, are also used in the service records. For those men who first saw operational service before 31 December 1915, and therefore received a 1914 Star or 1914/15 Star as well as the British War and Victory Medals, the numerical codes used differ slightly from those used for men who only saw their first operational service from 1 January 1916 onwards.

Pre 31/12/1915	Post 1/1/1916	
1	1	Western Europe
		a France and Belgium
		b Italy
2	2	Balkans
		a Greek Macedonia, Serbia, Bulgaria and European Turkey
		b Gallipoli (Dardanelles)

	3	Russia (4/5 August 1914 – 1/2 July 1920)
3	4	Egypt

    a 4/5 November 1914 – 18/19 March 1916
    b 18/19 March 1916 – 31 October/1 November 1918

4   5   Africa
    a East Africa, Nyasaland and Northern Rhodesia
    b South West Africa
    c Cameroon
    d Nigeria
    e Togoland

5   6   Asia
    a Hejaz
    b Mesopotamia
    c Persia
    d Trans Caspia
    e South West Arabia
    f Aden
    g Frontier regions of India
    h Tsing-Tau

6   7   Australasia
    a New Britain
    b New Ireland
    c Kaiser Wilhelmland
    d Admiralty Islands
    e Nauru
    f German Samoa

For more details relating to these operational theatres, see Joslin, Litherland and Simpkin, *British Battles and Medals*, pp 230–31.

10.2.2.4 Regimental order of precedence

For a comprehensive list of all regiments in order of precedence, see Joslin, Litherland and Simpkin, *British Battles and Medals*.

1 Life Guards	Royal Horse Artillery
2 Life Guards	1 Dragoon Guards
Royal Horse Guards	2 Dragoon Guards
Household Battalion	3 Dragoon Guards

4 Dragoon Guards
5 Dragoon Guards
6 Dragoon Guards
7 Dragoon Guards
1 Dragoons
2 Dragoons
6 Dragoons
5 Lancers
9 Lancers
12 Lancers
16 Lancers
21 Lancers
The Yeomanry Regiments
Royal Artillery
Royal Field Artillery
Royal Garrison Artillery
Royal Engineers
Royal Flying Corps
Grenadier Guards
Coldstream Guards
Scots Guards
Irish Guards
Welsh Guards
Royal Scots
Queen's Regt (Royal West Surrey)
Buffs (East Kent)
King's Own Regt
Northumberland Fusiliers
Royal Warwickshire Regt
The Royal Fusiliers
The King's (Liverpool Regt)
Norfolk Regt
Lincolnshire Regt
Devon Regt
Suffolk Regt
Somerset Light Infantry
Prince of Wales's Own (West Yorkshire Regt)
East Yorkshiere Regt
Bedford Regt
Leicester Regt
Royal Irish Regt
Yorkshire Regt (Green Howards)

Lancashire Fusiliers
Royal Scots Fusiliers
Cheshire Regt
Royal Welch Fusiliers
South Wales Borderers
King's Own Scottish Borderers
Cameronians (Scottish Rifles)
Royal Inniskilling Fusiliers
Gloucester Regt
Worcester Regt
East Lancashire Regt
East Surrey Regt
Duke of Cornwall's Light Infantry
Duke of Wellington's (West Riding Regt)
Border Regt
Royal Sussex Regt
Hampshire Regt
South Staffordshire Regt
Dorset Regt
Prince of Wales Volunteers (South Lancashire Regt)
Welsh Regt
Black Watch (Royal Highlanders)
Oxfordshire and Buckinghamshire Light Infantry
Essex Regt
Sherwood Foresters (Notts and Derby Regt)
Loyal North Lancashire Regt
Northamptonshire Regt
Princess Charlotte of Wales's (Royal Berkshire Regt)
Queen's Own (Royal West Kent Regt)
King's Own Yorkshire Light Infantry
Shropshire Light Infantry
Duke of Cambridge's Own (Middlesex Regt)
King's Royal Rifle Corps
Duke of Edinburgh's (Wiltshire Regt)
Manchester Regt
Prince of Wale's (North Staffordshire Regt)

York and Lancaster Regt
Durham Light Infantry
Highland Light Infantry
Seaforth Highlanders
Gordon Highlanders
Queen's Own Cameron Highlanders
Royal Irish Rifles
Princess Victoria's (Royal Irish
   Fusiliers)
Connaught Rangers
Princess Louise's (Argyll and Sutherland
   Highlanders)
Prince of Wales's Leinster Regt
Royal Munster Fusiliers
Royal Dublin Fusiliers
Rifle Brigade
Machine Gun Corps
Royal Tank Corps
Labour Corps
Royal Army Chaplains Department

Royal Army Service Corps
Royal Army Medical Corps
Royal Army Ordnance Corps
Royal Army Veterinary Corps
Honourable Artillery Company
The Territorial Force units
Monmouthshire Regt
Cambridgeshire Regt
London Regt
Inns of Courts Officers Training Corps
Hertfordshire Regt
Herefordshire Regt
Northern Cyclist Bttn
Highland Cyclist Bttn
Kent Cyclist Bttn
Huntingdon Cyclist Bttn

10.2.2.5 Other campaigns

The only other campaign medal which men of the RFC won was Khedive's Sudan Medal 1910, the roll of which is in WO 100/407.

10.2.3 *Royal Naval Air Service*

The First World War campaign medal rolls for members of the RNAS can be found in ADM 171. ADM 171/89–91 contains the medal roll for officers and ADM 171/94–119 contains the medal roll for RN ratings. The roll for men of the Royal Marines can be found in ADM 171/167–171. In many cases, although the name of an individual may be found in the medal rolls, the entry says that the medal(s) may have been issued by the Air Ministry (AM). Although there are no Air Ministry Medal Rolls (see Section 10.3.4), details regarding what medal(s) a man received can be found on his record of service. See Chapter 6 for further details.

All of the First World War medal rolls are arranged in alphabetical order. The entry can provide surname, first name and initial, service number, rank, which medal(s) the individual was entitled to (abbreviated to 14ST for 1914 Star, C meaning clasp for the 1914 Star, ST for 1914/15 Star, B for British War Medal and V for Victory Medal) and how the medals were disposed of (where they were sent).

A separate roll for the 1914 Star awarded to naval personnel can be found in ADM 171/139. There are no Silver War Badge rolls for men of the RNAS.

Medal rolls for campaigns involving the Fleet Air Arm are still held by the Naval Medal Office. See Appendix 2 for further details.

10.2.4 Royal Air Force

As such there are no specific First World War campaign medal rolls for the RAF in any AIR record class. All of the data relating to men of the RFC can be found in WO 329 and that of RNAS men in ADM 171.

In many cases men who qualified for at least a 1914 Star or 1914/15 Star serving in any regiment or corps of the army apart from the RFC, prior to transfer, may have a Medal Index Card (WO 372). Men who qualified for just a British War and Victory Medal whilst serving in any regiment or corps of the British Army apart from the RFC, prior to transfer, may also have a Medal Index Card (WO 372). Men who only saw operational service in the RAF after 1 April 1918 will probably not have a Medal Index Card (WO 372).

The only way to verify the medal entitlement of many men who saw service in the Royal Air Force only during the First World War is to look at their records of service. See Chapter 7 for more details.

Apart from the Silver War Badge (SWB) records for the RFC in WO 329, the only true RAF record relating to the SWB can be found in AIR 2/197/C33296.

10.2.5 Post-1918 campaigns

Although the RAF has been involved in a number of different operations for which campaign medals were awarded for service since 1918, the PRO only has the medal roll for one of these campaigns. Some details relating to post-1918 campaign medals may be found on records of service. See Section 7.2.2.

Operations against the 'Mad Mullah' in Somaliland in January and February 1920, by a number of DH 9as of Z Unit, resulted in the award of the African General Service Medal with the Somaliland 1920 clasp to just over 200 members of the RAF. The medal roll for this award can be found in AIR 2/2267–2270. All other post-1918 campaign medal records apart from this exception are still held by the Ministry of Defence. See Appendix 2 for further details.

10.3 Awards for gallantry and meritorious service

Beyond medals awarded for just being there are awards for gallantry and meritorious service. Those individuals who performed acts of gallantry or who carried out their normal tasks above the standards normally expected could receive official recognition of such deeds, in the form of additional awards.

All awards to British nationals were announced in the *London Gazette* (see Section 10.4). Many of these announcements were accompanied by citations (a brief explanation relating to the circumstances of the award) and many were not. It is the surviving recommendations for the honours and awards which you need to find in order to discover the story behind these awards.

Awards to foreign nationals who served in the RFC and RAF did not usually appear in the *London Gazette* and consequently the recommendation for the award should be sought. There are plenty of files in AIR 2 concerning awards to these men.

10.3.1 *Royal Engineers Balloon Section*

Prior to the First World War, and indeed the formation of the RFC, only a small number of officers and only two men (Sgt W.H. Pearce and Sgt W.J. Wellman, both of No. 1 Balloon Section, who received the Distinguished Conduct Medal [*London Gazette*, 26 June 1902]) of the RE Balloon section were decorated for services in the Boer War. Records relating to the deeds for which these men were decorated are not easily found. Apart from looking at the Royal Engineers' history, a copy of which is available in the PRO Library, the only likely record sources available are the South African War papers in WO 108, War Office Registered Papers: General Series in WO 32 Code 'O' AU and Code 50, Submissions for the Distinguished Conduct Medal in WO 146 and the announcements which appear in the *London Gazette* in ZJ 1.

10.3.2 *Royal Flying Corps*

The most important thing to remember when researching gallantry and meritorious awards won by members of the RFC is that the RFC was a corps of the British Army. Therefore any awards won by men of the RFC prior to April 1918 are likely to be army awards.

The Victoria Cross (VC) (which could be awarded to both officers and other ranks) was and still is the highest award for gallantry in the face of the enemy. Prior to the creation of the RAF's own specific awards in 1918 (see Section 10.3.4) the

Distinguished Service Order (DSO) and the Military Cross (MC) were the only other awards available to recognize acts of gallantry by officers.

For other ranks, apart from the VC, the only other awards available to recognize acts of gallantry were the Distinguished Conduct Medal (DCM) and from 1916, the Military Medal (MM).

Due to the complex nature of the statutes of the DSO, MC, DCM and MM, it was in fact possible for them also to be awarded for distinguished service, as well as just for gallantry in the face of the enemy.

From 1916 the Meritorious Service Medal (MSM) was awarded to a number of men for gallantry, not in the face of the enemy, but primarily for good service above that normally expected. List of names of men awarded the MSM were published in the *London Gazette*.

The lowest form of official recognition was a Mentioned in Despatches (MiD). Although a recipient did not receive a separate medal for this, he was entitled to wear a bronze oakleaf on the Victory Medal ribbon, signifying that he had been Mentioned in Despatches. Recipients of an MiD also received a certificate giving the name of the recipient, whose despatch they were mentioned in, and the date on which their name was published in the *London Gazette*.

All awards for gallantry and meritorious service were announced in the official state newspaper, the *London Gazette*. Many of the announcements were accompanied by brief citations describing the deed for which the award was granted. See Section 10.4 on how to use the *London Gazette*.

Fuller descriptions of the deeds for which honours and awards were granted may be found in files concerning recommendations for such awards. The majority of surviving recommendations for honours and awards are in the record class AIR 1. There are no general sections within AIR 1 where these files may be found. They are distributed throughout the whole class. To find many of these files it helps if you know which squadron or wing an individual was serving in at the time of the award, as this can help you limit the number of files you need to look at. A few of the files which contain recommendations for honours and awards are listed below.

- Recommendations for honours and awards. RFC in the field. August – October 1916
  AIR 1/993/204/5/1216
- New Years honours Gazette correspondence. September 1917 – February 1919
  AIR 1/1479/204/36/131
- Honours and awards. December 1917 – May 1918

AIR 1/1522/204/67/19
- Honours and awards. June 1917 to January 1919
  AIR 1/1526/204/68/19
- Recommendations for honours and awards: HQ RFC France. October 1915
  AIR 1/2147/209/3/131

You can look for honours and award files in AIR 1 using two methods:

1. Do a keyword search on the computerized catalogue, using such search terms as honour(s), award(s), recommendation, decoration(s) and the squadron number if you know it.
2. Search the AIR 1 card index, available in the Research Enquiries Room, using similar terms to those listed above. The card index will provide you with the original Air Historical Branch (AHB) reference for a file, which can then be used with the AIR 1 class list to identify the full PRO document reference.

Other record sources concerning honours and awards include:

- WO 389 The DSO and MC Gazette Book, which includes citations similar to those which appear in the London Gazette, many of which are annotated with further details
- WO 390 Register of the DSO
- WO 391 Register of the DCM and WO 388 Register of Foreign Awards.

All of these records are available on microfilm in the Microfilm Reading Room.

Card indexes listing those men who were awarded the DCM, MM or MSM are available in the Microfilm Reading Room. Each index provides name, rank, service number and unit details, and notes the date on which the award was announced in the *London Gazette*. WO 389/9–24 contains an alphabetical list of all those commissioned and warrant officers awarded the Military Cross (MC). Each entry provides name, rank, unit and *London Gazette* date.

The PRO Library has a large number of books concerning honours and awards and those who received them. All of the most important books about honours and awards are listed in the bibliography including the DFC roll, DFM roll and the DSO 1886–1923.

10.3.3 Royal Naval Air Service

As the Royal Naval Air Service was administered by the Admiralty, its members were awarded naval gallantry awards.

As already mentioned, the ultimate reward for gallantry was, and still is, the Victoria Cross. Only two members of the RNAS were awarded the VC. Flight Lieutenant Rex Warneford was awarded the VC for destroying the German zeppelin LZ37 on 7 June 1915, the award being gazetted on 11 June of the same year. Squadron Commander, later Vice Admiral, Richard Bell-Davies was awarded the VC for rescuing a colleague who had been shot down near Ferejik Junction, Bulgaria, on 19 November 1915, the award being announced in the *London Gazette* on 1 January 1916. Bell-Davies's flight report for this incident can be found in AIR 1/649/17/122/421.

Naval aviators and others serving in the RNAS were eligible for a number of different awards, including the Distinguished Service Order (DSO), Distinguished Service Cross (DSC), Conspicuous Gallantry Medal (CGM) and Distinguished Service Medal (DSM). A Naval Meritorious Service Medal (MSM) was instituted in January 1919, with many retrospective awards being made for service in the First World War.

Much as with the RFC, there are a number of different record classes containing details concerning honours and awards granted to members of the RNAS.

The most important record collection relating to honours and awards granted to officers and warrant officers of the RNAS is the collection of 'Honours Sheets' in ADM 171. These sheets contain much detail which does not appear in the *London Gazette*. The 'Honours Sheets' are in ADM 171/78–88 and are arranged by sheet identification letter and page number. A nominal card index providing sheet and page number of those who appear within the sheets is available in the Microfilm Reading Room.

Beyond the 'Honour Sheets' there are a number of other record classes of both the Admiralty and Air Ministry where further files concerning honours and awards may be found.

Admiralty correspondence in ADM 1, ADM 116 and ADM 137 contains files relating to honours and awards. These three record classes can all be searched using the Admiralty Index and Digest in ADM 12. Searches of ADM 12 can be made either for the individual using the alphabetical indexes or by using the numerical 'Digest' code indexes. The 'Digest' codes worth using are 85a Honours and Rewards or 90 Aviation. Apart from 1914, there are two volumes of ADM 12 for each part of the alphabet or range of 'Digest' numbers for the period 1915–19, each of which needs to be searched. A 'How to Use ADM 12' leaflet is available upon request from the desk in the Research Enquiries Room.

Once again a keyword search on the computerized catalogue may provide some references. See How to Use the PRO for further details.

The only piece of ADM 116 which relates specifically to RNAS honours and awards is ADM 116/1560 Honours and Awards for service during the period ending 31 December 1917.

As the RNAS combined with the RFC to form the RAF, a large number of files concerning RNAS honours and awards are also to be found in AIR 1. See Section 10.3.2 for information about using AIR 1. These files include, for example, AIR 1/75/15/9/173, RNAS Dunkerque Command – Honours and awards gained by officers and men, 1916–19.

All awards for gallantry or meritorious service were announced in the *London Gazette*, with citations accompanying many awards. For information about the *London Gazette*, see Section 10.4.

A number of very useful books concerning the DSC and DSM are available for consultation at the PRO. *Fringes of the Fleet* by Richard Witte about the DSC and *The Distinguished Service Medal 1914–1920* by W.H. Fevyer both contain useful information.

Rolls of the CGM, DSM and Naval MSM can be found in ADM 171/61. A roll of the CGM and DSM is in ADM 171/75. A roll of the CGM can also be found in ADM 1/25295.

A roll of foreign orders awarded to naval officers can be found in ADM 171/67.

Names of naval officers submitted for appointment to the Order of the British Empire can be found in ADM 171/135–137.

10.3.4 Royal Air Force in the First World War

The creation of the RAF on 1 April 1918 brought with it the need for new honours and awards for the new service. The Distinguished Flying Cross, Air Force Cross, Distinguished Flying Medal and Air Force Medal were all instituted in June 1918, details of which can be found in AIR 2/59 and ADM 1/8511/15. Thus before the end of the war it would be possible to see officers and men of the RAF wearing Army and RAF honours and Navy and RAF honours.

Sources concerning awards granted to officers and men of the RAF can be found in AIR 1, within the units' records and in AIR 30, Submissions to the Sovereign. Although the majority of recommendations for awards are in AIR 1, a number of files may also be found in AIR 2, Series A, Code 32/1 and AIR 2, Series B, Code 30.

Amongst the records in AIR 1 are:

- RAF Honours and awards August 1918 – April 1919
  AIR 1/107/15/9/287
- Record of Honours awarded: Unit index book July – November 1918
  AIR 1/878/204/5/584

10.3.5 Royal Air Force between the wars

Between 1919 and 1939 officers and men of the Royal Air Force were decorated for their gallantry not only in operational flying but also for numerous pioneering flights around the world. Files can be found in AIR 2, Series A, Codes 32/1 and 32/2, AIR 2, Series B, Code 30, AIR 5 and AIR 8.

The majority of surviving recommendations for awards for gallantry in operations can be found amongst the records relating to those operations. See Section 8.4.2 for further details. Recommendations for awards for operations in Somaliland in 1920 can be found in AIR 2/204. Files containing recommendations for long distance flights in 1919 and 1920 can be found in AIR 2/110 and AIR 2/119. Recommendations for awards to the crew of the airship R33 in 1925 can be found in AIR 2/277.

Bravery awards connected with the R101 airship disaster are recorded in AIR 2/8783.

The long distance flights from Egypt to Australia were recognized with awards, details of which can be found in AIR 2/4022.

Awards for service in Mesopotamia (later Iraq) between 1918 and 1920 can be found in AIR 2/2841. A file concerning awards for services in the Penjwin area of Iraq in 1927 can be found in AIR 5/222.

Operational awards for service in Waziristan in 1937 and 1938 can be found in AIR 2/2516, 3803, 9393 and 9404. Awards for service in Palestine immediately prior to the Second World War can be found in AIR 2/9404.

Citations for a number of operational awards were published in the *London Gazette*. See Section 10.4 for further details.

Submissions to the Sovereign in AIR 30 also contain some brief details relating to awards granted between the wars.

10.3.6 Royal Air Force in the Second World War

Owing to the changing nature of warfare in the Second World War, it is not surprising to find that one of the most common gallantry awards between 1939 and 1945 was for gallantry in the air: the Distinguished Flying Cross (DFC), of which over 20 000 were awarded.

The majority of files containing recommendations for awards granted to RAF personnel in the Second World War are in AIR 2, Series B, Code 30, AIR 2 Numerical Lists and some in WO 373, most notably WO 373/47 and 105.

There were different categories as well as types of awards bestowed upon men and women of the RAF and WRAF. Awards for flying were split into both operational and non-operational, and also into immediate awards (those requiring recognition of a specific act or acts within a short period) or non-immediate awards (recognizing courage over a longer given period, usually a tour of operations). Gallant acts on the ground, rescuing aircrew from crashed aircraft, for example, were also recognized, as were acts of meritorious service in support of operations.

Files relating to flying awards granted to personnel of the army and navy who served with the RAF may also be found in AIR 2. The RAF also controlled the committee which oversaw the award of the George Cross (GC), George Medal (GM) and the British Empire Medal (BEM). Consequently it is possible find these awards made to soldiers and sailors as well as airmen.

Numerous awards were granted for some of the most famous air operations between 1939 and 1945. Awards for the Battle of Britain can be found in AIR 2/4086, 4095, 8351 and 9468. The recommendation for the only Victoria Cross won during the battle can be found in AIR 2/5686.

As there are so many files relating to awards granted between 1939 and 1946 it helps to know when the award was announced in the *London Gazette* and/or the original Air Ministry file reference containing the recommendation.

A typical example of an RAF recommendation for awards can be seen in Figure 19.

10.3.6.1 Nominal indexes of RAF gallantry and meritorious service awards

There are several hundred files concerning honours and awards granted for services in the Second World War. Unless you have certain details which can help you narrow your search, you may have to look at a number of different files before you find the information you seek. You may be able to find the details you need in two indexes containing information which can enable a researcher to find the correct AIR 2 file.

CONFIDENTIAL

RECOMMENDATION FOR HONOURS AND AWARDS

Christian Names ....Geoffrey............   Surname......Silva...........

Rank ....Pilot Officer............   Official Number.AUS402258.....

Command or Group ..92 Group............   Unit....24 O.T.U.............

Total hours flown on operations.....160........

Number of sorties.............21..............

Recognition for which recommended.....DFC.......

Appointment held......Screened Instructor.......

Particulars of meritorious service for which the recommendation is made, including date and place.

On 31.7.42 P/O Silva was Captain of Whitley V. BD 327 engaged in a raid on Dusseldorf. The aircraft was severely attacked by very accurate Flak and was held in a searchlight cone in the target area. P/O Silva pressed home his attack and bombed the target from 13000'. The wireless operator was wounded in the leg and the rear turret was hit and could not be turned. Shortly after leaving the target the aircraft was attacked by a night fighter which raked the whole length of the fuselage with its fire. The ailerons and rudder were shot away and a fire broke out in the fuselage. Pilot Officer Silva gave orders to his crew to abandon aircraft, and he himself baled out at 10000'. By this time the whole fuselage was ablaze and he only had time to attach his parachute by one hook and dive through the flames. He was burnt in the face, neck and wrists, and his Mae West and harness were on fire. A few seconds after leaving, he saw the aircraft explode in the air. On landing near Charleroi, P/O Silva had to help the wireless operator on account of his wound and more or less carried him on his back through the night. P/O Silva and his wireless operator eventually arrived at Gibraltar and were brought home together. The officer has no previous decoration.

Date....2/10/42........   Signature of Commanding Officer....*SBarnes*....

Rank.....*Gp Capt*.....

Remarks by Air or other Officer Commanding:-

A very stout effort for a pilot "resting" at an O.T.U.! Recommended

HAHames

Date........4/10/42......   Rank......................

Air Commodore,
Commanding No. 92 Group. R.A.F.

Figure 19 Typical example of an RAF award recommendation (AIR 2/4910)

The Honours section at RAF Innsworth has a nominal index which can provide the reference to the Air Ministry file in which details relating to a given award were originally placed. Many of these files no longer exist and only the PRO records what survives. The original Air Ministry file reference still needs to be converted into a PRO document reference, so that the file can be ordered on the computer. Only original recipients or their next of kin will be provided with details by RAF Innsworth (see Appendix 2).

The second nominal index has been compiled over many years by recording all of the names of individuals who appear in the *surviving* AIR 2, Series B, Code 30 honours files, and then putting them into a computer. Many awards were down-graded; many recommendations were unsuccessful. Many individuals were recommended for honours more than once and the computerized index covers all these entries. All awards for gallantry and meritorious service, from the Victoria Cross to Mentioned in Despatches, from Knight Commander of the Order of the Bath to British Empire Medal, are listed, as are awards to foreign nationals and awards from foreign states to British nationals. For further details about this index contact: Paul Baillie, 14 Wheatfields, St Ives, Huntingdon, Cambridgeshire, PE17 6YD, telephone 01480 465691, e-mail paul.baillie@talk21.com.

10.3.7 *Fleet Air Arm in the Second World War*

Surviving recommendations for honours and awards to members of the Fleet Air Arm can be found in a number of different record classes. The class containing the most is ADM 1, Series 1, Code 85, with further awards within the same class under ADM 1, Series 2, Code 85 and ADM 1 'Numerical List'. With the advent of on-line keyword searches, it is possible to find the necessary files, as long as you know the name of the ship, squadron or operation. As with the award files in AIR 2, not all of the Admiralty award files have survived.

When a number of files relating to a specific subject were compiled, they were sometimes turned into case files. These case files can be found in ADM 116, and the relevant files relating to awards can be found in ADM 116, Code 85. A small amount of files concerning awards can also be found in the operational records in ADM 199. The recommendation for the award of a posthumous Victoria Cross to Temp. Lt R.H. Gray RCNVR can be found in ADM 1/24300. Amongst other honours and awards (H&A) files in Admiralty record classes are:

- Awards for the sinking of the *Bismarck*.
  ADM 1/11260
- Awards for attacks on German warships *Scharnhorst*, *Gneisenau* and *Prinz Eugen*.
  ADM 1/12459 and 12460

- Awards to personnel of aircraft carriers *Formidable*, *Furious* and *Indefatigable* for air attacks on the *Tirpitz*.
  ADM 1/16695
- Report on the Fleet Air Arm attack on the *Tirpitz* and recommendations for awards.
  ADM 116/5648

10.3.8 Glider Pilot Regiment and Army Air Corps

The nature of the job men of the GPR and AAC performed was such that they might receive gallantry awards for service both in the air and on the ground. As this is the case it is possible to find recommendations for awards in AIR 2, Series B, Code 30 and in WO 373. The majority of awards for gallantry whilst flying are in AIR 2, and those for gallantry on the ground are in WO 373. Apart from a specific policy file concerning the process by which men of the GPR could be recommended for flying awards, the recommendations for awards are distributed amongst the award files in AIR 2. A full list of the awards gained by men of the GPR can be found in *The History of the Glider Pilot Regiment* by Claude Smith.

Of the awards for post-1945 operations, flying awards to army personnel for service in Korea can be found in WO 373/119 and similar awards for service in Malaya 1951–60 can be found in WO 373/136.

10.3.9 Royal Air Force since 1945

Awards granted to members of the RAF continued to be announced in the *London Gazette* as they still are today. The surviving files containing recommendations for awards are primarily to be found in AIR 2, Series B, Code 30 and the AIR 2 'Numerical List'. It is also possible to identify surviving files by using the 'On-line Lists'.

Of the surviving post-war files a number are worth noting:

Reference	Operation
AIR 2/9986	Berlin Airlift
AIR 2/16814	Recommendations for Malaya, June 1950 onwards
AIR 2/16185	Recommendations for Korea, December 1950 onwards
AIR 2/12276	US awards to RAF personnel in Korea, 1951
AIR 2/12423	Kenya, 1953–5
AIR 2/12424	Kenya, 1955–6
AIR 8/2125	Operation Musketeer, Suez, 1956
AIR 2/17390	Operations in South Arabia, 1964

10.3.10 *Fleet Air Arm since 1945*

Although personnel of the Fleet Air Arm have been involved in numerous operations around the world since 1945, the number of files containing the recommendations for awards is very few. Surviving honours and awards files for the post-1945 period can be found in ADM 1, Series 2, Code 85, ADM 1 'Numerical List' and ADM 116, Code 85. With the advent of on-line searching, locating possible files should be easier.

10.4 The *London Gazette*

The *London Gazette*, founded in 1665, is the official government newspaper containing acts of state, proclamations and appointments to offices under the crown. All military appointments and announcements relating to commissions into the armed forces, promotions and announcements relating to awards for gallantry and meritorious service or Mentioned in Despatches are published in the *London Gazette*. The paper is published periodically throughout each month of the year. The page numbering is sequential from the beginning of the year to the end. At the end of each quarter (March, June, September and December), half year (June and December) or end of year (December), indexes are published which list the various subjects and names of individuals which have appeared in the paper during a given period.

Index volumes for the periods 1914–21 and 1940–46 are available in the Microfilm Reading Room. Each year of these indexes is split into quarters. All other indexes need to be identified in the *London Gazette* (ZJ 1) class list and ordered on the computer.

In order to find the particular entry for an individual, you need to have certain information which will enable you to find the correct edition. It will help if you have any of the following: name, rank and unit, type of award and the approximate date.

Prior to 1942, each section of a *London Gazette* index concerning honours and awards was arranged in alphabetical order by name of award, and then the list of names of recipients in alphabetical order, each name with a page number. After 1941, rather than be split into various sections representing each different honour, the *London Gazette* indexes were split into sections headed: Honours and Distinctions; Mentioned in Despatches; and Commendations.

As each index represents a given part of the year, for example, a quarter, the page number relating to an individual will appear within that period. Once you have identified the page number where an announcement is located, apply the page number to the *London Gazette* (ZJ 1) class list and order that volume of the *London Gazette* which has the page number in it.

10.5 Long service awards

Long service and good conduct medals (LSGCs) were and still are awarded to military personnel with an unblemished career over a given period. This period varied according to the service into which an individual entered. The various types of awards issued by different services are described below.

10.5.1 Army issue

The LSGC awarded to members of the RE Balloon Section, 37 members of the RFC and 8 members of the RAF, was awarded for 18 years' unblemished service. The medal rolls for the army issue LSGC can be found in WO 102. With the creation of the RAF in 1918, members of the RAF became eligible for their own award – see Section 10.5.3.

10.5.2 Royal Navy issue

Men of the RNAS and Fleet Air Arm had to have served for at least 15 years with unblemished conduct in order to qualify for the LSGC. The medal rolls for the RN issue LSGC are in ADM 171. Only ADM 171/73 contains the names of men of the RNAS who were awarded the medal. Other LSGC rolls are in ADM 171/140–145 and ADM 171/149–159. As the Fleet Air Arm still exists, this medal is still being issued.

Men of the Fleet Air Arm who served in the Royal Fleet Reserve (RFR) and who went on to qualify for the RFR LSGC may be found in ADM 171/160–163.

10.5.3 Royal Air Force issue

Announced in Air Ministry Weekly Order 520 of 1918 and instituted by Royal Warrant on 1 July 1919, the RAF LSGC was awarded for 18 years served with unblemished conduct. The ribbon of this medal, half crimson and half navy blue, with white edges, represents its army and navy counterparts, signifying the origins of the RAF. As the award was made retrospective from 1 April 1918, it was possible for men who had seen initial service in the army and navy prior to transfer into the RAF to qualify for this award also. Awards of the RAF LSGC were announced in Air Ministry Weekly Orders (AMWOs) between 1919 and 1941, and between 1950 and 1964. Some AMWOs can be found in AIR 72. The RAF Museum at Hendon has a complete run of AMWOs (see Section 15.6 for more detail).

A bar signifying a further award of the medal was authorized in 1944. In 1947 the medal was made available to officers promoted from the ranks as long as they had served 12 years in the ranks. In 1977 all three services standardized the length of service needed to be awarded an LSGC medal to 15 years.

Examples of the George V period RAF LSGC can be seen in Figure 20.

10.5.4 *The Air Efficiency Award*

The Air Efficiency Award was instituted in September 1942 and was awarded to both officers and men for 10 years' efficient service in the Royal Auxiliary Air Force and Royal Air Force Volunteer Reserve. Officers who received this award were permitted to place the letters AE after their name.

The Air Efficiency Award has recently been replaced by the Volunteer Reserves Service Medal.

Figure 20 The RAF Long Service and Good Conduct
medal. Left, obverse. Right, reverse. The medal on the
left also has a clasp on the ribbon denoting a further award.

11 | Courts martial

As the Royal Air Force was formed from parts of the two other services, it is necessary to look briefly at the courts martial records created by the Admiralty and War Office, as well as the records created by the Air Ministry.

Many records of courts martial are closed for up to 100 years. Consequently, although the date of a particular court martial may be known, obtaining more than brief details may be restricted by what is available

11.1 Admiralty records

There are really only two Admiralty record classes which contain details about courts martial for the period 1908–18, when aviation was in its infancy in the Royal Navy. These classes are ADM 1 and ADM 156. If an individual was tried by court martial, there may be an annotation on his record of service (see Chapter 6). In order to find any proceedings or further details concerning the case, it may be necessary to consult the alphabetical section of the Admiralty Index and Digest in ADM 12. A brief guide on how to use ADM 12 can be obtained from the Research Enquiries Room desk.

11.2 War Office records

War Office courts martial records are many. However the arrangement of the most important records concerning the RE Balloon Section and RFC means only a small number may need to be consulted, as explained below.

The Judge Advocate General's (JAG) Office charge books are held in WO 84 and the Registers of Courts Martial are in WO 92 and WO 213. These records are arranged in chronological order. In the case of WO 213 the date given in the registers is the date when the information was received by the JAG. The trial may have taken place a number of weeks before the information was received in London.

Registers of District Courts Martial between 1829 and 1971 can be found in WO 86. These records are similar to those in WO 213, showing the name, rank and regiment of the accused, together with the place of the trial, charge and sentence.

Similar records to those in WO 86 but concerning courts martial held abroad and covering the period 1779–1960 can be found in WO 90. The same sort of records, but covering India only, between 1878 and 1945, are in WO 88.

11.3 Air Ministry records

Policy papers relating to courts martial can be found in AIR 2, Series A, Code 21, AIR 2, Series B, Code 28, AIR 2 'Numerical List' and AIR 20, Code 28. There are also five AIR classes which hold JAG Office records dealing specifically with courts martial of RAF personnel:

Reference	Type of record
AIR 18	Proceedings
AIR 21	Registers
AIR 43	Charge books
AIR 44	Minute books
AIR 71	Out-letter books

AIR 18 comprises 134 files and covers the period 1941–94. It contains the proceedings of district, general and field general courts martial of RAF officers and airmen.

AIR 21 comprises 10 volumes and covers the period 1918–65. These registers give name and rank of each prisoner, place of trial, the nature of the offence and the sentence. If an individual was tried by court martial, it is to these registers that you should turn first:

- District courts martial, home and abroad, April 1918 – March 1938
  AIR 21/1A
- Field general courts martial, abroad, April 1918 – April 1947
  AIR 21/1B
- General courts martial, abroad, May 1918 – December 1960
  AIR 21/2
- General courts martial, home, June 1918 – December 1960
  AIR 21/3
- General courts martial, abroad, May 1927 – August 1937
  AIR 21/4A
- District courts martial, home, April 1938 – November 1942
  AIR 21/4B
- District courts martial, abroad, May 1938 – October 1942
  AIR 21/4B
- District courts martial, WAAF, home, May 1938 – April 1945
  AIR 41/4B

- District courts martial, home, November 1942 – January 1945
  AIR 21/5
- District courts martial, abroad, November 1942 – March 1947
  AIR 21/5
- District courts martial, WAAF, home and abroad, January 1945 – April 1964
  AIR 21/5
- District courts martial, home and abroad, January 1945 – March 1948
  AIR 21/6
- District courts martial, home, February 1948 – June 1954
  AIR 21/7
- District courts martial, home and abroad, March 1954 – December 1965
  AIR 21/8

The charge books in AIR 43 are very similar to those in WO 213 and are arranged in date order. These charge books provide information on each individual's name, rank, unit, offence, place of trial and the sentence if found guilty.

The minute books in AIR 44 contain details sent to the Judge Advocate General concerning legal aspects, precedents and irregularities, which arose from various RAF courts martial. These records are arranged in chronological order.

The Judge Advocate General's Office Out-Letters in AIR 71 are similar in nature to the records in AIR 43 and AIR 44.

12 Prisoners of war and war crimes

Although members of the British armed forces have been captured in a number of different conflicts, this chapter deals exclusively with those men who fell into enemy hands between 1914 and 1918, and between 1939 and 1945.

12.1 First World War

Records relating to men captured between 1914 and 1918 are scarce. Although the PRO does not have an exhaustive list of those captured, some details relating to the date and circumstances of capture do survive.

Records of casualties, including those men missing who were subsequently reported as prisoners, can be found amongst the unit operational records in AIR 1. These records include RFC, RNAS and RAF personnel. As far as is known, no records in any Admiralty record class, beyond annotations on records of service, show which members of the RNAS were captured. The total number of members of the RNAS who were captured up to 31 March 1918 was 118 – see AIR 1/109/15/18.

A number of files in WO 161 '1914–1918 War: Miscellaneous Unregistered Papers' contain repatriation reports made by returning prisoners of war after they arrived back in the United Kingdom. The reports in WO 161/95–101 contain details relating to these prisoners' capture, and in many cases mention the names of other individuals who were either captured at the same time or whom the prisoners encountered during their captivity. This collection is only a sample as it does not contain details of all those who had been prisoners of war.

Records of debriefs of escaped airmen can also be found in AIR 1/501/15/233/1.

Officers captured during the First World War had to submit a report on the circumstances of their capture when they were repatriated at the end of the war. Many of these reports survive for officers who served in most arms of the British army, in the individual's records of service (see Chapter 5).

The PRO does have a published list of officers captured between August 1914 and November 1918. *List of British Officers taken Prisoner in the Various Theatres of War.*

August 1914 – November 1918 (London Stamp Exchange, reprint 1988) is available in the Microfilm Reading Room. The Royal Air Force list, including the RFC, starts on page 146. The RNAS list starts on page 176. The whole work is indexed.

The only other source held by the PRO which may contain an indication of prisoner of war status is the annotation 'P of W' or 'POW', sometimes found on a Medal Index Card (see Chapter 10).

12.2 Second World War

The dominant role of aircraft during the Second World War not surprisingly led to large numbers of men of the flying services falling into enemy hands. Records held by the PRO relating to prisoners of war held by the Axis powers are numerous. However, some are not as detailed as others. Many records relating to prisoners of war, prison camps and war crimes can be found in AIR 2 Code 89 and AIR 20 Code 89.

12.2.1 Lists of prisoners

There are a number of sources, outlined below, containing basic details of those men, and in some cases women, who were held prisoner at any time between 1939 and 1945.

WO 392 'Prisoner of War lists: Second World War', contains lists of those individuals held by Germany, Italy and Japan. These lists provide name, rank, service number, prisoner number and which camp an individual was held in.

WO 345 'Japanese Index Cards of Allied Prisoners of War and Internees' are arranged in alphabetical order and contain basic biographical and service data, together with date of capture and the camps in which individuals were imprisoned. Cards which have been crossed through with red lines indicate a prisoner who died in captivity. Further nominal rolls of prisoners held by the Japanese can be found in AIR 49/ 383–388.

AIR 20/2336 is an alphabetical list of all RAF and Dominion aircrew held by the Germans in 1944–5 and provides service details and where individuals were held.

AIR 40/1488–1491 contains nominal rolls of those men held in Stalag Luft III and Stalag IIIA. Stalag Luft III was the camp from which the 'Great Escape' was made in March 1944. Seventy six officers escaped, of whom fifty who were recaptured were subsequently executed on Hitler's orders – see Section 12.3.

The PRO also has a number of published prisoner of war lists available in the Microfilm Reading Room.

12.2.2 Prisoner of war camp records

A number of camp histories can be found in WO 106 'Director of Military Operations and Military Intelligence, and predecessors: Correspondence and Papers', WO 208 'Director of Military Operations and Intelligence and Director of Military Intelligence: Files' and AIR 40 'Directorate of Intelligence'. These histories contain details of some individuals who were imprisoned, but they are primarily concerned with details about the camp, its organization and location. AIR 14/461–465 contains details of German camps.

12.2.3 Escaped prisoners of war

A number of men during the Second World War managed to either narrowly evade capture or indeed escape from those holding them. Once again the records relating to these men are not complete, but the records that are available do provide some very interesting details.

The most important collection of records is the MI 9 debrief records, completed by escapees and evaders when they returned to the United Kingdom. Many of these records can be found in WO 208 Directorate of Military Intelligence papers, under the references WO 208/3297–3327 and 3348–3352. Other examples of these can be found in AIR 14/2072–2073 and AIR 40/1533 and 1545–1552.

12.2.4 Repatriated prisoners of war

Once again a number of different sources can provide details about airmen captured during the war. AIR 14/469–471 contains reports into the circumstances of capture of RAF aircrew as do AIR 14/1233 and 1864. Records in WO 208/3328–3347 also contain similar information.

A detailed description of RAF POW escape organizations, together with a list of men of the RAF who were captured, can be found in WO 208/3244 and 3245.

12.2.5 Honours and awards

A number of individuals who either escaped or who evaded capture and returned to allied lines were rewarded for their fortitude and gallantry. Many of the MI 9 records in WO 208 and AIR 40 are annotated with details relating to the rewards these men were given. As their deeds were performed on the ground, it is not surprising to find that these men were awarded either the Military Cross or Military Medal, depending upon rank.

Apart from the annotated records in WO 208 and AIR 40, it is also possible to find recommendations for awards in AIR 2, Series B, Code 30, in files titled 'Ground Gallantry' and also in WO 373, in either the 'Escape and Evasion' section or in the section titled 'The London Omnibus List for Gallant and Distinguished Services in the Field'.

Files concerning men recommended for awards for their actions in POW camps can be found in AIR 40/1488 Stalag Luft III East, AIR 40/1490 Stalag Luft III Belaria, and AIR 40/1491 Stalag IIIA. An example of such a recommendation, that for the award of a Military Cross to Flt Lt O.L.S. Philpot RAF, who was involved in the 'Wooden Horse' escape, can be found in WO 373/95 (ff35–ff45).

For further details on honours and awards, see Chapter 10.

12.3 War crimes

The execution of fifty of the officers who took part in the 'Great Escape' (see Section 12.2.1) was not the only instance of a war crime committed against RAF and Dominion personnel during the Second World War.

Records relating to war crimes are distributed amongst a number of different record classes. The most useful way to approach this subject is to consult in the Research Enquiries Room the guide, *War Crimes Records in the PRO Originating in the Ministry of Defence: Alphabetical List of Locations etc*. This contains numerous references relating to specific war crimes, their investigation and in some cases the prosecution of the perpetrators.

Documents concerning the 'Great Escape' can be found in AIR 2/10121, AIR 40/266, 268, 270, 285, 287, 2265, 2293, 2313–2314 and 2487, WO 32/15502 (Code 91A), WO 208/2901 and 3441, and WO 311/135, 169–182 and 599.

War crimes documents concerning Operation Freshman can be found in WO 309/720, WO 311/383, 386, 387 and WO 331/16, 17 and 18.

13 Medical records

This chapter is concerned with those medical records which are not held with records of service.

13.1 Records up to the end of the First World War

Records relating to aviation medicine prior to the Second World War are not common. Medical records concerning men of the flying services up to the end of the First World War were primarily created by various service medical organizations, such as those involved in the treatment of battle casualties or in the general medical care of individuals in peace and in war.

13.1.1 ADM 101 Surgeon's Journals

Apart from a few annotations which occur on the records of service of naval officers and RNAS officers in ADM 196 and ADM 273 respectively, and naval ratings records in ADM 188, details relating to individual medical case papers do not exist.

All ship's surgeons had to complete a daily log noting basic details relating to the medical cases they had seen on each day. The majority of records in ADM 101 are for RN warships, but there are a number of logs which either concern ships which are known to have carried aircraft or were kept at Royal Naval Air Service or Fleet Air Arm shore establishments. The following journals are a few examples which can be found in this record class:

Reference	Title	Date
ADM 101/311	Flying School, Eastchurch	Jan – Aug 1914
ADM 101/314	HM Air Station, Isle of Grain, Kent	Jan – Dec 1914
ADM 101/316	HM Aviation Service, Expeditionary Force	Aug – Dec 1914
ADM 101/332	RN Armoured Car Division	Mar – Dec 1915
ADM 101/338	Naval Air Station, Calshot	Jan – Dec 1915
ADM 101/371	RN Airship Detachment No. 2	Jul – Dec 1915
ADM 101/372	RNAS Expeditionary Force, France	Jan – Feb 1915
ADM 101/390	No. 4 Wing RNAS, France	May – Dec 1916
ADM 101/390	No. 5 Wing RNAS, France	Mar – Dec 1916

ADM 101/392	RN Air Station, Redcar	Mar – Dec 1916
ADM 101/393	RN Air Station Vendome, France	Aug – Dec 1916
ADM 101/394	RN Flying School, Eastchurch	Jan – Mar 1916
ADM 101/439	Chingford Air Station	1917
ADM 101/439	Crystal Palace Air Station	1917
ADM 101/441	Dunkirk Air Station	1917
ADM 101/441	Aircraft Depot, France	1917
ADM 101/442	Pulham Air Station	1917
ADM 101/443	Redcar Air Station	1917
ADM 101/443	Tresco Air Station	1917
ADM 101/444	Tipnor Kite Balloon School	1917
ADM 101/444	Vendome Air Station, France	1917
ADM 101/468	Withnoe Air Station	1918

13.1.2 MH 106 1914–1918 War: Representative Medical Records

The Medical Historian's papers in MH 106 consist of a 2 per cent sample of all of the British Army and therefore RFC medical records generated between 1914 and 1919.

The majority of the records concern non RFC and RAF personnel. However, a number of files deal specifically or partly with sick or wounded of either the RFC or RAF. Most of the records are hospital and casualty clearing station admission books and general casualty records which cover a variety of different parts of the British Army. There are, however, a number of RFC medical sheets relating to both officers and men of the corps who were either wounded or sick in MH 106/2202–2206. These records, dated 1916–17, can provide name, rank, number and unit, and a description of the ailment for which the individual was hospitalized:

MH 106/2202	Surnames A–C
MH 106/2203	Surnames D–H
MH 106/2204	Surnames I–O
MH 106/2205	Surnames P–S
MH 106/2206	Surnames T–Z

Admission and other records in MH 106, which include details relating to men and women of the RFC, RNAS, RAF and WRAF, can be found in:

14 Field Ambulance
| MH 106/59 | Royal Air Force | May – Dec 1918 |

51 Field Ambulance
| MH 106/121 | Royal Air Force | Aug 1918 |

66 Field Ambulance

MH 106/153	Royal Air Force	Jun – Sep 1918
MH 106/154	Royal Air Force	Jun – Oct 1918

139 Field Ambulance

MH 106/205	Royal Air Force	May – Sep 1918

3 Casualty Clearing Station

MH 106/392	Royal Air Force other ranks	Jun 1918 – Jan 1919
MH 106/393	Royal Air Force other ranks	Jul 1918 – Jan 1919

11 Casualty Clearing Station

MH 106/513	Royal Air Force	May 1918 – Mar 1919

31 Casualty Clearing Station

MH 106/645	Royal Air Force officers	Jun – Dec 1918
MH 106/647	Royal Air Force officers and other ranks	Mar – Sep 1919
MH 106/652	Royal Air Force other ranks	May – Jun 1918
MH 106/665	Royal Air Force	Aug – Sep 1918

34 Casualty Clearing Station

MH 106/742	Royal Air Force officers and other ranks	Jun – Dec 1918
MH 106/760	Royal Naval Air Service	May – Jul 1917
MH 106/793	Royal Air Force	Jun 1918 – Jan 1919
MH 106/794	Royal Air Force officers and other ranks	Jul 1918 – Jan 1919

39 Casualty Clearing Station

MH 106/810	Royal Air Force	May – Dec 1918
MH 106/811	Royal Air Force	Jan – Mar 1919

2 General Hospital

MH 106/987	Royal Naval Air Service	Feb – Mar 1918
MH 106/1029	Royal Air Force	Jul – Dec 1918
MH 106/1030	Royal Air Force officers and other ranks	Jan – Mar 1919
MH 106/1034	Royal Air Force other ranks	May – Jun 1918
MH 106/1035	Royal Air Force officers	Jul – Dec 1918
MH 106/1037	Royal Air Force officers and other ranks	Jan 1919

18 General Hospital

MH 106/1139	Royal Flying Corps	Jul 1917 – Jan 1918

MH 106/1140	Royal Flying Corps	Jul – Aug 1917
MH 106/1141	Royal Flying Corps	Aug 1917
MH 106/1143	Royal Flying Corps	Sept – Oct 1917
MH 106/1145	Royal Flying Corps	Oct – Nov 1917
MH 106/1146	Royal Flying Corps	Nov – Dec 1917
MH 106/1147	Royal Air Force	Dec 1917 – Dec 1918
MH 106/1148	Royal Flying Corps & Royal Naval Air Service	Feb – Mar 1918
MH 106/1149	Royal Flying Corps	Mar 1918
MH 106/1153	Royal Flying Corps	Apr 1918
MH 106/1156	Royal Air Force	Apr 1918
MH 106/1157	Royal Air Force	Apr – May 1918
MH 106/1164	Royal Air Force	Jun 1917 – Jan 1919
MH 106/1180	Royal Air Force other ranks	May 1918 – Jan 1919
MH 106/1187	Royal Air Force	Oct 1917 – Mar 1918

19 General Hospital

MH 106/1235	Royal Flying Corps	Apr – May 1916
MH 106/1238–1258	Royal Flying Corps	Sept 1916 – Apr 1918
MH 106/1259	Royal Air Force	Apr 1918
MH 106/1260	Royal Air Force	Apr – May 1918
MH 106/1261	Royal Air Force	May – Jun 1918
MH 106/1264	Royal Flying Corps	Apr – Jun 1916
MH 106/1265	Royal Flying Corps	Jun – Jul 1916
MH 106/1266	Royal Flying Corps	Jul – Oct 1916
MH 106/1269	Royal Flying Corps	Nov 1916 – Mar 1917
MH 106/1270	Royal Flying Corps	Nov 1916 – Jun 1917
MH 106/1281	Royal Air Force	Mar – Dec 1918
MH 106/1284	Royal Flying Corps	Nov 1915 – Jun 1917
MH 106/1288	Royal Flying Corps	Jun 1916 – Dec 1917
MH 106/1290	Royal Flying Corps	Sep 1916 – Aug 1917
MH 106/1291	Royal Flying Corps	Aug – Dec 1917
MH 106/1292	Royal Flying Corps	Jan – Nov 1918

28 General Hospital

MH 106/1316	Royal Flying Corps	Aug 1916
MH 106/1318	Royal Flying Corps	Aug 1916
MH 106/1322	Royal Flying Corps	Sep 1916
MH 106/1333	Royal Flying Corps	Mar – Apr 1917
MH 106/1335	Royal Naval Air Service	Apr – May 1917
MH 106/1337	Royal Flying Corps	May – Jun 1917
MH 106/1339	Royal Flying Corps	Jun 1917
MH 106/1340	Royal Flying Corps	Jun – Jul 1917
MH 106/1365	Royal Flying Corps	Nov 1915 – Oct 1916

| MH 106/1368 | Royal Air Force officers and other ranks | Jun 1918 – Apr 1919 |

85 General Hospital

| MH 106/1381 | Royal Air Force | Jan – Aug 1919 |

4 Stationary Hospital

MH 106/1460	Royal Flying Corps	Oct – Nov 1916
MH 106/1483	Royal Air Force	Feb – Apr 1918
MH 106/1491	Royal Air Force	1918 – 1919
MH 106/1494	Royal Air Force officers	Jun 1918 – Sep 1919
MH 106/1497	Women's Royal Air Force	Apr – Sep 1919

County of Middlesex War Hospital at Napsbury

MH 106/1528	Royal Air Force	Mar 1918 – Jun 1919
MH 106/1529	Royal Air Force	Nov 1918 – Jul 1919
MH 106/1530	Royal Air Force	May 1918 – Apr 1919

Queen Alexandra's Military Hospital Millbank

MH 106/1636	Royal Air Force	Apr – Dec 1918
MH 106/1637	Royal Air Force officers	Apr – Dec 1918
MH 106/1638	Royal Air Force cadets and other ranks	Jan – Apr 1919
MH 106/1639	Royal Air Force officers	Jan – May 1919
MH 106/1690	Royal Air Force	Jun – Aug 1917
MH 106/1691	Royal Air Force	Aug – Oct 1917
MH 106/1692	Royal Air Force	Oct – Dec 1917

Catterick Military Hospital

| MH 106/1825 | Royal Air Force officers and other ranks | Jun 1918 – Dec 1919 |
| MH 106/1899 | Royal Air Force officers | Jan 1918 – Feb 1919 |

Craiglockhart Hospital

MH 106/1900	Royal Air Force	Jul 1918 – Jan 1919
MH 106/1901	Royal Air Force	Aug 1918
MH 106/2037	Royal Air Force other ranks	Jun – Jul 1918

31 Ambulance Train

| MH 106/2038 | Royal Air Force officers | Jun – Jul 1918 |
| MH 106/2040 | Royal Air Force other ranks | Jul 1918 – Apr 1919 |

13.2 AIR 49 Reports used for the Official History of the RAF Medical Services 1939–45

This record class contains records created by the Air Ministry, covering all aspects of medicine in the Royal Air Force. Most of the records are concerned with general medical policy and medical studies, rather than individuals, but it is possible to find people mentioned in a number of files. For example, the history of RAF Hospital Wroughton in AIR 49/322 contains the names of key staff in an appendix at the end of the file. Medical histories of various RAF units can be found in this class but they are concerned with the medical state of a unit and the types of cases which occurred in that unit only.

14 Photographs

As a photograph archive the PRO holds some very rare and unusual photographs connected with aviation. Although there are images of numerous individuals, these are usually in unnamed groups rather than named portrait type photographs.

The variety of images the PRO holds is reflected in the 'In Camera' books which have been published by Sutton Publishing. Although not all of the photographs have come from the PRO, these guides do show what is likely to be found. Another rich source is the PRO's *RAF in Action 1939–1945: Images from Air Cameras and War Artists*, written by Roy Conyers Nesbit and published in April 2000.

There are numerous different record classes where photographs may be found. Those that have been discovered have been listed in a photograph catalogue which can be found in the Research Enquiries Room.

A number of photographs have been extracted from their original homes and placed into new collections. Photographs extracted from AIR record classes have been put into the record class CN 5, and those extracted from the AVIA record classes have been put into CN 6.

It is possible to find photographs of famous individuals. Beyond looking in the photograph catalogue, you can use an individual's surname as part of a keyword search on the 'On-line Lists'.

Many operational records contain photographs of the results of aircraft action. The ORBs of training units in AIR 29 contain many course photographs of trainee aircrew.

For more advice about the photographic holdings of the PRO you may wish to contact staff in the Image Library.

15 Records held by other institutions

15.1 Fleet Air Arm Museum

The Fleet Air Arm museum at Yeovilton houses the greatest collection of aircraft, archives and artefacts connected with British naval aviation, anywhere in the world. Many of the aircraft on display are unique to Europe, and many are the sole example of their type in the world.

For those interested in research into aircraft and personnel of the RNAS and FAA, the museum has an unrivalled collection, which continues to grow. Indeed the archival staff assisted me with my own research, for which I am most grateful.

The museum can be contacted at:

Fleet Air Arm Museum
RNAS Yeovilton
Ilchester
Somerset
BA22 8HT

Tel: 01935 840565

Website: www.faam.org.uk

15.2 Royal Engineers Museum

The corps museum of the Royal Engineers houses numerous displays about all aspects of the life and history of the corps. Included in the displays, as one might imagine, are those concerning aviation, not only from the balloon era but also into the late 20th century. Also included in the displays is an unrivalled collection of medals awarded to members of the corps.

The RE Museum is at:

Brompton Barracks
Prince Arthur Road
Gillingham
Kent
ME4 4UG

Tel: 01634 8222261

15.3 Museum of Army Flying

Found at the home of the Army Air Corps, at Middle Wallop in Hampshire, this museum is primarily concerned with Army aviation in the 20th century. Displays concerning both the Glider Pilot Regiment and Air Observation Posts, together with those concerning the post-1957 Army Air Corps, are to be found in the museum along with examples of related aircraft and gliders. The museum has a library and archive where it is possible to research various aspects of army aviation. Enquiries concerning the archives should be made to the curator on tel: 01980 674339.

The address of the museum is:

Museum of Army Flying
Middle Wallop
Stockbridge
Hampshire
SO20 8DY

Tel: 01264 384421

Website: www.flying-museum.org.uk

15.4 Airborne Forces Museum

The Airborne Forces Museum at Aldershot in Hampshire houses various displays concerning the activities of troops of the British Army who arrived at their area of operations by air. Consequently the displays contain numerous items concerning the Glider Pilot Regiment.

The museum can be found at:

Airborne Forces Museum
RHQ The Parachute Regiment
Browning Barracks
Aldershot
Hampshire
GU11 2BU

Tel: 01252 349619

15.5 Imperial War Museum

The Imperial War Museum (IWM) which was founded in 1917 not only displays a wide variety of items concerning warfare in the 20th century but also holds extensive archives. Split into a number of different departments the IWM holds a vast array of archival material which may be of use to a researcher. Departments of Documents, Printed Books, Photographs and Sound may all provide the researcher with further information. The IWM is also responsible for the former RAF airfield at Duxford in Cambridgeshire. To obtain further details about access to the IWM contact:

Imperial War Museum
Lambeth Road
London
SE1 6HZ

Tel: 020 7416 5000

Website: www.iwm.org.uk

15.6 Royal Air Force Museum

The Royal Air Force Museum was opened in 1972 and contains displays from the earliest days of Army aviation in the 19th century to date. The library and archive of the museum holds a wide range of material relating to personnel of the RFC and RAF. By far the most important collection relating to pilots is the collection of photographs of holders of Royal Aero Club certificates.

Beyond the photographs, there are collections of casualty records for the First and Second World Wars, and a collection of Air Ministry Bulletins which contain basic biographical data relating to members of the RAF who received awards between 1939 and 1959.

For information about access to the archives contact the Department of Research and Information Services. The RAF Museum is located at:

Royal Air Force Museum
Graham Park Way
Hendon
London
NW9 5LL

Tel: 020 8205 2266

Website: www.rafmuseum.org.uk

15.7 Commonwealth War Graves Commission

The Commonwealth (formerly Imperial) War Graves Commission is responsible for the care and maintenance of cemeteries and memorials concerning the dead, primarily of the two world wars. The Commission holds most of its records on computer and the information they contain can be obtained either by writing to the Commission or by accessing its website.

The Commission is at:

The Commonwealth War Graves Commission
2 Marlow Road
Maidenhead
Berkshire
SL6 7DX

Tel: 01628 634221

Website: www.cwgc.org.uk

Appendix 1: RAF ranks

Commissioned ranks

RNAS 1912–18	RFC 1912–18 & RAF 1918–19	RAF 1919 – Present day	WAAF & WRAF 1939–67[1]
	General	Marshal of the Royal Air Force[2]	
	Lieutenant General	Air Chief Marshal	
	Major General	Air Marshal	Air Chief Commandant
	Brigadier	Air Vice-Marshal	Air Commandant
Wing Captain	Colonel	Air Commodore	Group Officer
Wing Commander	Lieutenant Colonel	Group Captain	Wing Officer
Squadron Commander	Major	Wing Commander	Squadron Officer
Flight Lieutenant	Captain	Squadron Leader	Flight Officer
Flight Sub-Lieutenant	Lieutenant	Flight Lieutenant	Section Officer[3]
	Second Lieutenant	Flying Officer	Assistant Section Officer[4]
		Pilot Officer	

Princess Mary's Royal Air Force Nursing Service[5] 1921–50	WRAF 1918–20	PMRAFNS 1951–80[6]
Matron-in-Chief	Commandant	Air Commandant
Chief Principal Matron[7]	Deputy Commandant	Group Officer
Principal Matron	Assistant Commandant I	Wing Officer
Matron	Assistant Commandant II	Squadron Officer
Senior Sister	Administrator	Flight Officer
Sister	Deputy Administrator	Flying Officer
Staff Nurse[8]	Assistant Administrator	

1 From 1 August 1968 WRAF officers had the same rank titles as their male counterparts: the WRAF was disbanded in 1994.

2 Introduced 1919 as Marshal of the Air; changed to Marshal of the Royal Air Force in 1925.

3 Changed to Flying Officer in 1949.

4 Changed to Pilot Officer in 1949.

5 Originally the Royal Air Force Nursing Service; became Princess Mary's in 1923.

6 From 1 April 1980, PMRAFNS officers have used the same rank titles as the RAF and WRAF, but the rank of Pilot Officer is not used.

7 In use between March 1944 and July 1948.

8 In use between January 1921 and June 1941.

Non-commissioned officers and airmen/airwomen

RNAS
Chief Petty Officer I
Chief Petty Officer II
Chief Petty Officer III
Petty Officer
Leading Mechanic
Air Mechanic I
Acting Air Mechanic I
Air Mechanic II

RFC
Warrant Officer
Quartermaster-Sergeant
Flight Sergeant
Sergeant
Corporal
Air Mechanic I
Air Mechanic II
Air Mechanic III

WRAF, 1918–20
Senior Leader
Chief Section Leader
Section Leader

Sub-Leader

Member

RAF, 1918
Sergeant Major I/Chief Master Mechanic/Chief Master Clerk
Sergeant Major II/Master Mechanic/Master Clerk
Flight Sergeant/Chief Mechanic/Flight Clerk
Sergeant/Sergeant Mechanic/Sergeant Clerk
Corporal/Corporal Mechanic/Corporal Clerk
——— /Air Mechanic 1st Class/Clerk 1st Class
Private 1st Class/Air Mechanic 2nd Class/Clerk 2nd Class
Private 2nd Class/Air Mechanic 3rd Class/Clerk 3rd Class

RAF, 1919–51[1]
Sergeant Major Class 1[2]
Sergeant Major Class 2[2]
Flight Sergeant
Sergeant
Corporal
Leading Aircraftman
Aircraftman 1st Class
Aircraftman 2nd Class

RAF, 1951–64[3]
Warrant Officer/Master Technician
Flight Sergeant/Chief Technician[5]
Sergeant/Senior Technician
Corporal/Corporal Technician
Senior Aircraftman/Junior Technician[6]
Leading Aircraftman

RAF, 1964 to date[4]
Warrant Officer/Master Aircrew
Flight Sergeant/Chief Technician[5]
Sergeant
Corporal
Senior Aircraftman/Junior Technician[6]
Leading Aircraftman

Aircraftman 1st Class
Aircraftman 2nd Class

Aircraftman

PMRAFNS 1963–71[7]
Chief Staff Nurse
Senior Staff Nurse
Staff Nurse 1
Staff Nurse
Student Nurse 1
Student Nurse 2
Student Nurse 3

PMRAFNS 1980 to date[8]
Warrant Officer
Flight Sergeant
Sergeant
Corporal
Senior Aircraftman
Leading Aircraftman
Aircraftman

AIRCREW RANKS 1946–50[9]
Master Aircrew
Aircrew I
Aircrew II
Aircrew III / Aircrew IV

[1] WAAF and WRAF ranks from 1939 on were similar to the male equivalents, e.g. Leading Aircraft*woman*.

[2] The rank of Sergeant Major was abolished in January 1933 and replaced by a single rank of Warrant Officer.

[3] & 4 NCOs and Airmen were placed into trade groups, and the Technician ranks were linked to trades involving technical skills, such as Engine Fitter and Musician. The traditional ranks were allocated to non-technical trades such as the RAF Regiment, Catering and Supply.

[5] Chief Technician is a stage *between* Sergeant and Flight Sergeant.

[6] Junior Technician is a stage *between* SAC and Corporal.

[7] Before 1963 all members of the PMRAFNS were commissioned. In March 1971 the PMRAFNS ranks were changed to followed the Technician structure in use at that time for male nurses serving in the RAF. In September of that year the Nursing trade group was split into two parallel schemes: those training as, or qualified as, State Registered Nurses followed the Technician route, whilst men and women qualified as or training as State Enrolled Nurses were allocated the traditional RAF ranks but were unable to rise beyond the rank of Sergeant.

[8] From 1 April 1980 all RAF nurses have followed the traditional rank structure.

[9] The rank titles used reflected the aircrew specialization, e.g. Master Pilot, Navigator III, Engineer II, etc. Aircrew under training had the rank of Cadet Pilot, etc. They proved unpopular and were dropped in favour of the Sergeant/Flight Sergeant system, with the exception of Master Aircrew which continues in use.

Appendix 2: Useful addresses

For useful addresses relating to museums and archives associated with aviation see Chapter 15.

Royal Air Force

Details of RAF officers and airmen whose records are not in the public domain and information about post-1920 medals can be obtained as follows:

Records of service:

PMA (CS) 2a2
Building 248a
HQ RAF PTC
RAF Innsworth GL3 1EZ

Medal records:

CS Sec 1d
Room F93
Building 256
HQ RAF PTC
RAF Innsworth GL3 1EZ

Fleet Air Arm (Royal Navy)

Details concerning naval officers and men of the Fleet Air Arm and post-1920 medals can be obtained from:

HMS Centurion
Grange Road
Gosport
Hampshire PO13 9XA

Army Air Corps

Details concerning officers and men of the Glider Pilot Regiment and Army Air Corps can be obtained from:

CS (R) 2b
Bourne Avenue
Hayes
Middlesex UB3 1RF

Details concerning post-1920 medals awarded to members of the British Army can be obtained from:

Army Medal Office
Government Office Buildings
Worcester Road
Droitwich
Worcestershire WR9 8AU

Appendix 3: Commonly found unit abbreviations in RFC/RAF service and related First World War records

The following is a list of abbreviations found in pre-1920 service records and other contemporary records relating to units of the RFC and RAF. There was no standard list of abbreviations to be used, and frequently more than one abbreviation for the same unit can be found in the same record. This lack of standardization also means that this list is far from exhaustive, but other abbreviations can often be deduced by using components of those found below. In the case of service records, the sequence of units can help (e.g. officers would be posted to a Cadet Wing or School of Aeronautics early in their service, and would often finish up at a Reserve Depot or Equipment and Personnel Depot). Details of support units of the RFC and RAF (i.e. anything except squadrons) can be found in *Royal Air Force Flying Training and Support Units* by R. Sturtivant, J. Hamlin and J.J. Halley. This volume also includes a place name index which can be useful in identifying unknown units, as place names are frequently found in early service records.

A&IC Sch	Artillery and Infantry Co-operation School
AAC	Air Ammunition Column
AAP	Aircraft Acceptance Park
ACMB	Aviation Candidates Medical Board
ACS	Airship Construction Station or Air Construction Service
AD	Aircraft Depot
AFC	Australian Flying Corps
AG & BS	Aerial Gunnery & Bombing School
Air Min	Air Ministry
AP	Aircraft Park
ARD	Aircraft Repair Depot
Arm Sch	Armaments School
ARP	Aeroplane Repair Park
ARS	Aeroplane Repair Section
ASC	Air Service Constructional (Corps)
ASD	Aeroplane Supply Depot
BCo	Balloon Company
Bde	Brigade
BEF	British Expeditionary Force
BTW	Balloon Training Wing
BTW	Boys' Training Wing
CCH	Casualty Clearing Hospital
CD	Clothing Depot
CDD	Cadet Distribution Depot
Cdt Brig	Cadet Brigade
CFC	Canadian Forestry Company
CFS	Central Flying School
CWg	Cadet Wing
DS	Depot Squadron
ELG	Emergency Landing Ground

EPD	Equipment & Personnel Depot
ETB	Eastern Training Brigade
FIS	Flying Instructors' School
FS	Fighting School
Gp	Group
GS	General Service(s)
HD	Home Defence
Hosp	Hospital
HQ	Headquarters
KB	Kite Balloon
KBS	Kite Balloon Section
KBT	Kite Balloon Training
Med Dist	Mediterranean District
Med Off Trg Sch	Medical Officers' Training School
MT	Motor Transport
MTD	Marine Training Depot
MTDpt	Motor Transport Depot
MTRD	Motor Transport Repair Depot
NF	Night Flying
NTS	Night Training Squadron
Obs Sch	Observers' School
OCW	Officer Cadet Wing
OTTW	Officers' Technical Training Wing
Pal Bde	Palestine Brigade
RAE	Royal Aircraft Establishment
RAF	Royal Air Force
RAS	Reserve Aeroplane Squadron
RD	Reserve Depot or Recruits' Depot
Rein Pk	Reinforcement Park
Res Sqdn	Reserve Squadron
RFC	Royal Flying Corps
RLP	Reserve Lorry Park
RS	Reserve Squadron
S of A	School of (Military) Aeronautics
S of F&G	School of Fighting & Gunnery
S of TT	School of Technical Training
SA	South African
SAD	Southern Air Depot
Sch for WO	School for Wireless Operators
Sch of AF	School of Aerial Fighting
Sch of AF & G	School of Aerial Fighting & Gunnery
Sch of AG	School of Aerial Gunnery
SD	Stores Depot
SDP	Stores Distributing Park
SEA	South East Area
SMA	School of Military Aeronautics
SNBD	School of Aerial Navigation and Bomb Dropping
Sqdn	Squadron
T	Training
TD	Tent Detachment
TDS	Training Depot Station
Trg Sqdn	Training Squadron
W or Wg	Wing
W&OS	Wireless & Observers' School
WEE	Wireless Experimental Establishment
WRAF	Women's Royal Air Force

Bibliography

Abbott, P.E. and Tamplin, J.M.A., *British Gallantry Awards* (Dix 1981)

Bowyer, C., *RAF Operations 1919–1939* (William Kimber 1988)

Carter, N. and C., *The Distinguished Flying Cross and How it was Won 1918–1995* (Savannah 1998)

Conyers, R. C., *RAF in Action 1939–1945: Images from Air Cameras and War Artists* (PRO 2000)

Escott, B., *Women in Air Force Blue: the Story of Women in the Royal Air Force from 1918 to the Present Day* (Patrick Stephens 1989)

Fevyer, W.H., *The Distinguished Service Cross 1901–1938* (London Stamp Exchange 1991)

Fevyer, W.H., *The Distinguished Service Medal 1914–1920* (Hayward 1982)

Fevyer, W.H., *The Distinguished Service Medal 1939–1946* (Hayward 1981)

Fowler, S. and Spencer, W., *Army Records for Family Historians* 2nd ed. (PRO 1998)

Halley, J.J., *Squadrons of the RAF and Commonwealth 1918–1988* (Air Britain 1988)

Henderson, D.V. Major (Retd) GM, *Dragons Can Be Defeated* (Spink 1984)

Henshaw, T., *The Sky Their Battlefield. Air Fighting and the Complete List of Allied Air Casualties from Enemy Action in the First World War* (Grub Street 1995)

Hobson, C., *Airmen Died in the Great War 1914–1918* (Hayward 1995)

Jefford, C.G. W/Cdr, *A Comprehensive Record of the Movement and Equipment of all RAF Squadrons and their Antecedents since 1912* (Airlife 1988)

Joslin, E.C., Litherland, A.R. and Simpkin, B.T., *British Battles and Medals* (Spink 1988)

Omissi, D., *Air Power and Colonial Control: The Royal Air Force 1919–1939* (Manchester 1990)

Raleigh, W. and Jones, H.E. *War in the Air* (HMSO). Regularly updated.

Rodger, N.A.M., *Naval Records for Genealogists* (PRO 1998)

Roskill, S., *Naval Policy between the Wars* (Collins 1968 and 1976, two volumes)

Seedies List of Fleet Air Arm Awards 1939–1969 (Ripley Registers 1990)

Shores, C. and Williams, C., *Aces High* (Grub Street 1994)

Shores, C., Franks, N., and Guest, R., *Above the Trenches: A Complete Record of the Fighter Aces and Units of the British Empire Air Forces 1915–1920* (Grub Street 1990)

Smith, C., *The History of the Glider Pilot Regiment* (Leo Cooper 1992)

Sturtivant, R., *Squadrons of the Fleet Air Arm* (Air Britain 1984)

Sturtivant, R. and Burrow, M., *Fleet Air Arm Aircraft 1939–1945* (Air Britain 1995)

Sturtivant, R. and Cronin, D., *Fleet Air Arm Aircraft, Units and Ships 1920–1939* (Air Britain 1998)

Sturtivant, R., Hamlin, J. and Halley, J.J., *Royal Air Force Flying Training and Support Units* (Air Britain 1997)

Sturtivant, R. and Page, G., *Royal Naval Aircraft Serials and Units 1911–1919* (Air Britain 1992)

Tavender, I., *The Distinguished Flying Medal: A Record of Courage 1918–1982* (Hayward 1990)

Tucker, N.G., *In Adversity – Exploits of Gallantry and Awards to the RAF Regiment and its Associated Forces 1921–1995* (Jade Publishing 1998)

Witte, R.C., *Fringes of the Fleet* (Nimrod Dix 1997)

Wynn, K.G., *Men of the Battle of Britain* (Gliddon Books 1989)

Useful periodicals

Aeroplane	Published monthly
Flypast	Published monthly
Cross and Cockade	Published quarterly and available from the PRO shop.

Index